Graduated... But Are You Ready to Succeed?

*Why So Many Grads Struggle—
And What You Need to Succeed After
College*

RAM V. IYER

Graduated… But Are You Ready to Succeed?

© 2025 Ram V. Iyer

All rights reserved by the author.

No part of this book may be reproduced, stored in a retrieval system, or transmitted in any form or by any means—electronic, mechanical, photocopying, recording, or otherwise—without the prior written permission of the author, except for brief quotations used in reviews or scholarly works, or as permitted under applicable copyright law.

Published by iAchiever Publishing,
an imprint of Business Thinking Institute LLC
Princeton, NJ. U.S.A.
www.iAchiever.org

Requests for permission, licensing, bulk purchases, translations, or limited educational/training use (e.g., excerpts, frameworks, handouts) should be directed to the publisher.

ISBN (Print): 979-8-9987517-2-1
ISBN (eBook): 979-8-9987517-3-8

First Edition

Disclaimer

This book is for informational purposes only. The author is not a doctor, therapist, or licensed mental health professional, and this content is not a substitute for professional advice. The strategies, stories, and ideas shared are based on personal experience, research, and interviews, and should be used at the reader's own discretion.

To my daughter
Anushka

TABLE OF CONTENTS

Before You Begin 11
*Why graduating doesn't mean you're ready—
and what this book will actually do for you*

I Know People Like You 17
One of Them Calls Me Dad

PART 1   THE REALIZATION 19
The disillusionment. Realization that school didn't prepare you.

1.   You Did Everything Right 21
2.   Resumes & Degrees Meet the Real World 29

PART 2   GETTING UNSTUCK 33
Letting go of old patterns, embracing imperfect action, building momentum.

3.   You're Playing the Wrong Game 35
4.   From Smart to Smartness 42
5.   First Steps Aren't Flashy or Certain 46
Interlude: I've Seen This Before 52

PART 3   BREAKING OLD PATTERNS 55

Core Smartness capabilities—judgment, self-direction, adaptability, relationships.

6. From Noise to Progress. 57
7. Breaking the Validation Addiction 62
8. Smartness Is Used Every Day and Everywhere 67
9. Shifting from Who You Were to Who You Need to Be 73
10. Dealing with Ambiguity 79
11. Using Your Learning Advantage 82
12. Joining The Tribe 86

Interlude: Certainty, Doubt, and the Real World 93

PART 4   BECOMING EFFECTIVE 95

Transition into ownership, action, and building a life of continuous loops and progress.

13. From Stumble to Stride. 97
14. From Learner to Guide 101
15. Discover What Fits 105
16. The Real Scorecard 109
17. Unlearning the School Rules 114
18. Smartness: The Planning Begins 118

PART 5 BUILDING MOMENTUM 121

Sustaining growth through continuous learning, reflection, and application.

19. Meeting at the Crossroads 123
20. It's on You Now 126
21. Ram's Gift 132
22. Takeoff 138
23. Six Months Later 142
24. The Real Beginning 144
Interlude: What Is a Successful Life? 145

Applying This Book in the Real World… Today 149
The Smartness Institute .153
Resources for Greater Success 154

More Praise for
Graduated… But Are You Ready to Succeed?

"This book is a wake-up call for high-achievers. Ram shows you how to convert your intelligence into real-world success."

— **Marc Ingram**, President,
Michigan Ross Alumni Club of Ann Arbor & Southeast Michigan

"This is the best book I've seen for the smart but underachieving—delivered with tough love and practical wisdom. I recommend it enthusiastically."

— **Chester Elton**, Bestselling Author of
The Carrot Principle and *Leading with Gratitude*

"Success doesn't come from being the smartest in the room—it comes from applying it smarter. This book shows you how."

— **Desh Deshpande**, Life Member, Governing Board of MIT
(Massachusetts Institute of Technology)

"If you've ever wondered why your intelligence and hard work haven't taken you further—this book explains why and provides a path to achieve greater success."

— **Larry Lifson**, Co-President,
Northwestern Kellogg Alumni Club of Chicago West

"We often focus so much on creating a better world that we forget to apply those same problem-solving skills to ourselves. Ram's approach gives you a way to become more well-rounded—and more successful."

— **Mark Johnston**, 2023–24 President, MIT Club of Washington DC

"Many smart people struggle to turn their potential into success. Ram delivers what seminars and shortcuts don't—a clear path forward and practical tools."

— **Don Huizenga**, Former President, World Foundry Organization

Before You Begin

"You explored the world around you as a child and teenager. Then you explored the world of books until graduation. Now it's time to learn how to succeed in the real world."

You've accomplished a major milestone in life: you've graduated from college. After years of lectures, group projects, cramming for finals, and pursuing a higher GPA, you've earned your degree. You've spent over 21 years studying hard: getting into honors classes, taking AP classes, chasing grades, getting into a good college... and graduated. Woohoo. You believed that all that work—literally a lifetime of effort—would lead to a good job and ready to take on the world. But if we're honest, "graduated" doesn't always feel like "ready."

You graduated. After years of chasing grades, passing exams, and doing everything right, you made it. Woohoo! You believed that all that work—literally a lifetime of effort—would prepare you for life. But if we're honest, 'graduated' doesn't always feel like 'life-ready', does it?

The transition from student to working professional is one of the most abrupt and poorly supported shifts in life. In school, there were clear rules, structured paths, and well-defined milestones. You had a rubric for most things! In the real world? There's no syllabus. No rubrics. No guaranteed feedback. No grades at the end of every quarter to tell you how you're doing. Just an open road ahead, full of uncertainty and unanswered questions.

Since childhood, you've been trained to use your intelligence. It helped you get good grades, strong test scores, a great college degree, and maybe even your first job. Intelligence got you this far. Your first job probably came because of your grades, your major, and your college—all measures of how well you leveraged your intelligence, not your ability to succeed in the real world. As a result, many new graduates believe that their intelligence, education and credentials will carry them for the rest of their lives. Many graduates think, "I've got a degree from school X. I'm all set." Except, you're not. You'll find out soon enough. Did school prepare you to succeed in the real world?

Even people with graduate degrees—MBAs, JDs, PhDs—often struggle in the real world, not because they aren't smart, but because they were trained for the classroom, not the uncertainty and demands of the real world.

School rewarded studying and scoring well. But the real world isn't a test. It rewards figuring things out, often without help or guidance. And it rewards capability—not just correctness.

Entry-level jobs aren't just disappearing because of AI. They're disappearing because few companies spend time or money training new hires. They expect you to arrive ready to deliver value on day one.

Smartness isn't something you're missing. You've been building it your whole life—from the day you were born—by navigating challenges, adapting and figuring things out. The difference now? You need to develop it intentionally and use it deliberately to get real results.

That's what Smartness gives you. Not just knowledge, but the ability to apply it in real-time. The sooner you develop your Smartness and leverage it effectively, the more valuable and employable you become.

Schools and colleges do little to prepare you for the real world. Yeah, I know. They claim they do. They don't. I've experienced it firsthand and also seen it with my daughter. As a result, you feel unprepared to enter the real world. You may be wondering,

What am I supposed to do now?
Am I falling behind?
Wasn't I supposed to feel more confident by now?

A few years ago, new grads had a clear edge in the job market. A degree was a door-opener. Now, for the first time in decades, recent graduates were actually more likely to be unemployed than the general population. The value of the degree hadn't vanished—but the guarantee had. A generation ago, a degree gave you a head start. Now, it felt like she was starting behind the line.

A regular college education doesn't prepare graduates for the real world. What else is required in order to succeed after graduation?

The world still celebrates the finish line, but real life doesn't begin with a handshake and a tassel turn. The world was telling graduates: "You've made it!"

Made it where? Made it for what?

You cannot 'connect the dots' looking forward. You can only prepare adapt to a range of potential situations. You need to have a way of preparing for an uncertain future. College doesn't prepare you for that. Formulas and rote knowledge are tools, not capabilities on how to use them in different situations. The college education system is not in sync with what graduates need after graduation.

Colleges don't want to let the hard truth get in the way of a good celebration.

College ends with graduation. Life just begins then.

This book exists because those questions are not signs of weakness, they're the starting point for growth. You're not lost. You're entering a new game with new rules. And what got you here—intelligence, credentials, effort—isn't enough by itself to get you where you want to go.

> *"You've checked all the college's requirements to graduate—but the world outside college plays by different rules. You need to learn to play that game to succeed in life."*

You're smart, and whether it feels like it or not, you're already advantaged. Only about 7% of the world's population holds a 4-year college degree. Whether you've just earned your bachelor's, your MBA, or another advanced credential, this book will help you turn your education (advantage) into real-world success.

In spite of all that, many smart people like you still struggle after graduation. Not because you aren't capable. But because you were trained to succeed in one system—school—where learning and test scores mattered most. Then, suddenly, you were thrown into another system—one where success depends on more than just intelligence. In the real world, it's about using your intelligence, and also your behaviors, choices, and ability to get results. That's where Smartness comes in.

Smartness is not about IQ. It's about how you apply your advantages—your intelligence, knowledge, capabilities, resources, assets, skills or something else—to navigate complexity, uncertainty, and opportunity to achieve desired organizational outcomes. Smartness is the ability to see things as they are, recognize what needs to be done, and take the right action. Smartness is a capability that anyone can learn. It's developed by cultivating mindsets, behaviors, habits, and skills that help you leverage your advantages, manage your disadvantages, and achieve greater success in the real world.

Smartness is not the same as intelligence. It's about how well you apply your intelligence or any other advantage. Smartness is what separates one's potential from achievement.

To succeed beyond college, you'll need to undergo a critical paradigm shift: from relying on intelligence, which helped you excel in the academic world, to developing Smartness, which enables real-world achievement. You need to shift from primarily accumulating knowledge and leveraging intelligence to the further development and leverage of Smartness. In school, being intelligent was enough to get you noticed, praised, and rewarded. But in the real world, intelligence is just the starting point. It's what you do with your intelligence that matters most.

Without this shift, you risk falling into what we call the *Smartness Gap*—the frustrating space between your potential and your actual results. You may see others with less talent moving ahead while you're still figuring out your direction and plan. The answer isn't to become smarter; it's to develop your Smartness.

In this book, you'll learn how to leverage and develop your Smartness to achieve real-world success. You'll uncover the hidden obstacles that hold new grads back. You'll build momentum toward your early-career goals. And you'll develop a mindset that gets sharper with every challenge.

As a college graduate, you've achieved something that remains relatively uncommon on a global scale. According to a study by Harvard University and the Asian Development Bank, only 6.7% of the world's population holds a college degree. In the United States, about 37% of adults aged 25 to 64 have a bachelor's degree or higher. This places you in a privileged group with significant advantages in the job market and beyond.

> *"Intelligence and your college education might help you avoid becoming a loser—but without Smartness, you'll never become an Achiever."*

As a graduate, your desire to succeed isn't in question. What's in question is whether you've developed the capabilities to succeed beyond college. Many graduates assume they already have what it takes—without ever developing or using their Smartness well. They may recognize pieces of it, but they haven't learned or mastered the full range of Smartness required to succeed.

So, if you're wondering, "How can I actually get ready for the real world?" this book is your guide.

You don't need to become more intelligent. You need to get smarter at leveraging who you already are, and what you already possess.

> *You're smart enough to graduate. Now, become smart enough to succeed in the real world.*

This book will show you how.

I Know People Like You
One of Them Calls Me Dad

You're smart. You've worked hard. You are probably mentally fatigued. You care about what comes next. You're looking forward to a real paycheck, a job that feels good, your own place, weekends to finally relax, and time to explore your interests. Maybe you've landed a job, maybe you're figuring it out, maybe you're quietly wondering, *Is this it? Am I behind already?*

I get it. One of the people I love most in this world has been going through the same situation.

My daughter is 24. She graduated from Vanderbilt and she's headed to Wharton for her MBA. She's already traveled to 48 countries across all 7 continents, lived in China and Singapore, worked at NASA and has a job she's excited about. From the outside, it looks like she's crushing it and has it all figured out. But I've seen what it's really like: the doubts, the pressure, the nonstop comparisons, the quiet fear that maybe she's not as ready as everyone thinks.

We've talked about how much life changes after graduation. How it gets messier, faster, and harder to measure. How being "smart" in the way school rewarded you—knowing the answer, acing the test, staying on the path—doesn't always help you once the path disappears.

No one teaches you what to do when your smarts aren't enough anymore. You're just expected to figure it out—even as the world keeps expecting greatness from you. But when life doesn't go as planned, you blame yourself or get pissed at the unfair world.

Here's what I believe:

> *Being smart helped you get here. But it isn't enough to get where you want to go.*

That's where Smartness comes in, a part most people are never taught. It's how you use what you've got: your perspective, behaviors, mindset, and ability to relate to others to make progress when things are uncertain. It's what can turn your potential into real results.

This book exists to help you do that. No fluff. No hype. No big promises. Just insights based on experience and data, accessible language that makes sense, and ideas that respect what you're already bringing to the table.

> *"You don't need to see the whole road. You just need to start walking."*

The real world is complex, and the competition is global. This book starts with the real world. And the real you. Right now.

PART 1

THE REALIZATION

The disillusionment. Realization that school didn't prepare you.

CHAPTER 1

YOU DID EVERYTHING RIGHT

Emma stood in line, cap slightly crooked, a thin smile frozen on her face. The air buzzed with camera clicks, cheers, and the occasional squeal from someone who had just spotted their name on the jumbotron. Around her, classmates looked radiant: grinning, hugging, broadcasting their next moves like awards: "Heading to NYC!" "Starting at Deloitte!" or "Got into grad school!"

Everyone kept saying the same thing: "You did it."

Emma kept nodding, thanking them, smiling back, but under the weight of the cheers and filtered photos, a single thought kept pressing against her chest. She had done everything right, and yet, instead of feeling ready, she felt exposed. Everyone made it sound like she'd arrived, but she couldn't shake the sense that she was stepping into something much bigger and more uncertain than anyone had warned her about.

Graduation was supposed to feel like a launch. She thought she'd feel powerful, clear, maybe even a little unstoppable. Instead, she felt like someone who'd just run a marathon only to realize the finish line was actually the entrance to an unfamiliar road. No route map. No syllabus. No real clue what came next.

Her phone buzzed. There was a new message in the family group chat. Her aunt had posted a stock photo of a graduation cap flying through the air with a caption in cursive: *"The future is yours!"*

Emma almost laughed. *Cool. But could someone please send me the instructions?*

The pressure to be excited was everywhere—on social media, in her family's voices, even in her own head. She had done what she was told. Pick a major. Go to class. Don't screw up. She got the degree. She landed the job. She followed the path. And now? Now she was *supposed* to feel ready. But what she actually felt was… hollow. Proud, sure. But also, weirdly anxious. Drained. A little lost.

> *"Being ready on paper doesn't mean you're ready off paper."*

She glanced around at the sea of gowns and families, wondering how many other people felt like this but were better at hiding it. She wasn't in crisis, just quietly unsure. Like she'd spent years climbing a staircase, only to reach the top and find a fog instead of a door.

Her parents hugged her like she'd just won an Oscar. Her younger cousin asked, "So what's next?" and Emma smiled and gave the usual line: "Starting a full-time role in marketing ops next month."

They beamed. "That's amazing."

She nodded. It should feel amazing. But beneath the smile, she felt a quiet unease. He friends and family were celebrating what she had just accomplished. But Emma couldn't stop thinking about what came next. And the more she thought about it, the more unsure she felt.

The job she had accepted sounded great on LinkedIn: solid company, decent salary, hybrid schedule. It looked like success. But inside, Emma couldn't shake the sense that she was not ready for it.

Back in her apartment that weekend, Emma sat on her bed in silence. She opened her laptop to check the onboarding email from her new employer. No butterflies. No spark. Just a checklist of tasks and logins. She scrolled. Read. Closed the tab.

She closed her laptop and lay back on the bed, staring at the ceiling. There was no sudden realization, no inspirational moment, just the quiet discomfort of not knowing what came next. She had expected to feel ready. Instead, she felt unsteady. That tension between how she appeared to everybody else, and how she actually felt lingered.

She was about to cross from the world she knew—college—and step into one she didn't. The real world. And that shift felt bigger than the ceremony made it seem. She didn't know if anyone else felt this way. Maybe they did. Maybe they were just better at hiding it. But deep down, Emma felt uneasy. Like she was standing on the edge of a major life transition, unsure how far the ground would stretch beneath her once she stepped forward.

She didn't have words for it yet, but part of her was beginning to sense it: graduation wasn't the end. It wasn't even a pause. It was the start of a life stage she didn't understand yet. There'd be no rubric. Just a wide-open space she didn't know how to navigate. This next part might be longer, messier, and far less certain than she'd been led to believe.

She had believed the hard part was behind her. The expectation was clear: graduate, start working, become an adult with a steady paycheck and a life that made sense. But as the celebration faded and her phone went quiet, a different feeling crept in. Not panic. Not excitement. Just a quiet uncertainty that left her feeling adrift, like she was stepping into a new phase in life where she didn't know the rules. She would be away from family, working with people she didn't know, answering to people she hadn't met, navigating expectations that no one had explained. Some of her support system, like friends, besties and family, may still be there, but only through texts, calls, or chats. Not across the hall. Not down the street. And definitely not in the office. Everything about the environment would be new, and she'd be expected to figure it out while proving she belonged. And she had to perform to earn the success she was seeking. She wasn't sure how.

She wasn't scared. Not exactly. But she couldn't shake the feeling that she was not prepared for that reality. And that maybe, just maybe, this next part was going to be much harder than anyone had told her. And somehow, she didn't feel ready or even sure what 'ready' looked like anymore.

"School ends with graduation; life does not."

School had taught her to study, to follow structure, to aim for the grade. But real life wasn't a classroom. She wasn't quite sure what it was yet. All she knew was that she needed something else: practical, real-world capabilities that she hadn't been taught in school. She knew that bookish knowledge and intelligence were not enough, but she didn't know exactly what those capabilities were, or how to develop and use them. She did know that if she wanted to succeed beyond graduation, she would have to figure them out.

Meanwhile, Jack didn't go to graduation. He told everybody that he didn't feel well, but the truth was simpler: he didn't feel like he had anything to celebrate as a graduate without a job. His name had technically been called, his degree confirmed and his transcript sealed. But it didn't feel like a milestone—just another day. A bad one, actually.

Jack didn't say it out loud, but part of the reason he skipped graduation was the pressure to look successful. Everywhere he looked: on social media, in alumni emails and even the commencement speaker lineup, he saw successful people with jobs and seemingly promising futures. Everyone seemed to be 'thriving'. Everyone seemed to have a plan. And Jack? He had questions he couldn't answer. Showing up meant stepping into a space built for people who already looked like they were successful.

It wasn't just about self-doubt. It was about visibility. Jack had started to notice a pattern—the more someone looked like they were crushing it, the louder their story was told, and the more visible they were. The university promoted them. Peers celebrated them. Families touted their achievements. And slowly, everyone else faded into the background. Jack was one of those ignored alumni. It wasn't that Jack didn't care. It's that nobody seemed to care about people like him who were smart, capable, but currently unemployed. He was relegated to the shadows. That's the quiet cost of success bias: a world where only the winners get noticed, making it seem like success is more common than it really is. That makes anyone who hasn't landed yet feel like they don't belong in the room.

He didn't think he belonged at the graduation ceremony. He didn't want to fake it. He didn't want to explain why he was unemployed. So, he stayed in his apartment, not out of apathy, but because showing up would've felt like walking into the wrong room. The successful room.

He stayed in his off-campus apartment, scrolling through Instagram stories of classmates in caps and gowns. "So proud of this chapter!" "Next stop: Google!" "Couldn't have done it without my people. XOXO." Jack was getting ready to move back in with his parents. His expectations of being independent and employed were shattered. He would be asking for a weekly allowance and have to share the family car—again! He had to explain his unemployment to his family, neighbors and friends, and so did his parents. He particularly hated having to face his aunt Nancy, a particularly judgmental and gossipy woman.

Jack watched it all with a strange blend of detachment and guilt. He wasn't bitter, not really. Just blank. He knew he should feel *something*. Motivated? Anxious? Inspired? Instead, everything inside him felt stuck in neutral.

He had applied to fifty-seven jobs. Gotten three interviews. One of them ghosted him after the final round. The other two sent polite rejections. The last one stung: "We were impressed by your background, but we've decided to move forward with other candidates." He had reread that sentence five times, wondering what part of his background wasn't impressive enough. GPA? Major? Too many internships? Not enough?

Last week, his dad had sent him an article from *The Atlantic*. The headline had made him wince:

"Something Alarming Is Happening to the Job Market—AI Is Replacing College Grads." The part that stuck with him the most? "College doesn't confer the same labor advantages it did 15 years ago."

He read that sentence three times. It sounded like a betrayal. Like everything he had believed—the idea that if you were smart, worked hard, and got a good degree, success would follow—were myths someone forgot to update. They were advantage illusions that were getting busted.

Even MBAs from schools like Harvard were struggling. Jack had read that nearly a quarter of their most recent class still didn't have jobs months after graduating. That number used to be in the single digits just a few years ago. If people with elite credentials and global networks were getting stuck, what chance did he have? He wasn't a Harvard grad. He didn't have a famous last name or a well-funded VC fellowship.

He had trained for work like drafting reports, analyzing data, and building presentations. But now, it was already being handed off to AI tools. No training. No salary. No hesitation. If a machine could think like him, and companies didn't want to train him, was he valuable? Was there a new skill or mindset he could acquire or develop that could make him more valuable?

He didn't have an answer. But for the first time, he realized he needed to start asking different questions.

He knew the job market was tough. Everyone said that. But deep down, Jack felt like something else was off. He just didn't know what that was. It was like there was a step everyone else had figured out that he hadn't even seen yet.

He had been told he was smart his whole life. In high school, in college, even during coffee chats with alumni. "You're thoughtful," someone once told him. "Analytical. You'll go far." But no one said how far he'd have to drift before he started going anywhere.

Most days now blurred together. Jack made to-do lists but rarely checked anything off. He convinced himself he was "figuring things out," but if he was honest, most of his time went to job boards, YouTube, and late-night gaming. He told friends he was "between opportunities." It sounded better than "I have no idea what I'm doing."

His roommate had already moved out. His lease was up in three weeks. And he still had no job, no solid plan, no real energy to chase either.

He wasn't spiraling. But he wasn't moving forward, either. And part of him had started to wonder: *If I'm so smart, why does everything feel stuck?*

It had been a week since his last interview. No reply. No update. Just silence. He refreshed his inbox. Still nothing. It was like the process had vanished with him in it.

He stared at the screen a little longer, trying to will a notification into existence. Nothing came. Just the hum of the mini fridge and the weight of not knowing.

That was the worst part, not the rejection, but the silence; and the silence felt like failure.

No one teaches you what to do when your smarts aren't enough. You're just expected to figure it out, even as the world keeps expecting greatness from you.

They didn't know each other yet. Emma and Jack had never met. But they were both walking the same edge, just from different angles. Emma, driven and high-performing, felt unsteady beneath the weight of success. Jack, cautious and unsure, felt invisible beneath the silence.

CHAPTER 2

RESUMES & DEGREES MEET THE REAL WORLD

Emma was excited about her new job. She showed up early on her first day—new laptop bag, crisp blouse, a little nervous but mostly proud. This was it. Her real adult job. No more late-night problem sets or group projects with freeloaders. She was in the big leagues now, and making the big bucks too.

The office was nice enough. Her onboarding manager was polite, the HR videos were fine, and the team seemed smart. But by the end of that first week, something strange had started to settle in.

No one cared that she'd graduated magna cum laude. Nobody asked about her thesis or how many internships she'd done. Most of the other new hires were just as credentialed. They joked about student loans, swapped onboarding hacks, and met for overpriced coffee. It was friendly. It just didn't matter.

Her manager gave her a generic project, a short deadline, and zero explanation. It wasn't personal, just how things worked. Everyone was busy. No one had time to handhold.

She felt it: the slow drop from "rising star" to "new hire." At school, her intelligence had been obvious, affirmed constantly. Here, it was invisible. And honestly? Irrelevant.

She wasn't failing but not standing out either. Her ideas got passed over in meetings. Her emails went unanswered. She second-guessed her tone, her speed, her value. She didn't want to seem entitled, but something wasn't adding up.

Wasn't I supposed to be ready for this? she kept thinking.

She had the job. But she wasn't taking off. She had just landed hard.

On the walk home that Friday, Emma replayed the week like a film she wasn't sure she liked. She hadn't messed up. She hadn't missed a deadline. But none of it felt like progress.

She pulled out her phone and texted a friend from college: *This week was weird. I feel… invisible.*

The reply came fast: *Lol, you're new. That's just how it is.*

Maybe. But the feeling lingered.

It wasn't imposter syndrome. It wasn't fear. It was a quiet, nagging realization: this job wasn't going to validate her the way school had. And success here wasn't going to show up just because she was smart.

She kept wondering if doing everything right was supposed to feel this uncertain. Wasn't hard work supposed to be enough? She showed up early, stayed late, asked questions, smiled through the awkwardness. Still, something felt off.

She walked on eggshells, always trying to read the room. Did her manager think she was doing a good job? Did her colleagues even notice her? She was doing everything she thought she was supposed to. She was eager, reliable and available.

She had a badge, a desk, and a title. But for the first time in a long time, none of it felt like it meant anything. The doubt crept in slowly. Maybe she wasn't as ready as she thought. Maybe she had been overhyped by her parents, her professors, and even herself. She didn't say any of that out loud. Not yet. But the silence around her? It was starting to speak louder than she expected.

No one teaches you what to do when you're not ready for the real world. You're just expected to figure it out, even as the world keeps expecting greatness from you. It's like being thrown into the deep end of the swimming pool. They just expect you to swim.

Jack – When Silence Bites

Jack had been ghosted before, but never like this. He'd made it to the final round. Spent hours preparing. Sent the thank-you notes. Even replayed the interview afterward and thought, *I didn't bomb that.*

But now it had been ten days. No call. No email. Just silence.

He checked his inbox like a ritual. Even opened the spam folder. Nothing. He reread his own follow-up email, second-guessing the tone: *Was I too eager? Too confident? Too much?*

Eventually, he stopped checking. But the silence remained.

That job wasn't just a job. It was supposed to be proof that he was on the right path. That all the effort had meant something. That he was getting traction. Instead, the silence made it feel like none of it had happened.

His parents tried to be helpful. "Just follow up again," they said. Or, "Maybe it wasn't a good fit."

Jack didn't want another polite dismissal. He didn't want encouragement, he wanted clarity. Feedback. Something he could work with. Instead, he got nothing. He wasn't just frustrated. He was angry: at the silence, at the system, at himself.

He had thought intelligence meant you'd always find your way. But what do you do when no one even tells you what road you're on?

He opened LinkedIn. Another classmate had just accepted a role at a VC firm. Another had launched a startup. Another posted a photo of his standing desk with the caption, *"Grind mode. Let's go."*

Jack closed the app. His own update would've read: *"Still waiting to hear back. Again."* So, no Jack update.

That night, he sat in his old bedroom, back at his parents' place, staring at a blank Google doc he'd labeled "Plan B." There he had no plan B. There was just more waiting. Or maybe, he thought, there was something he hadn't learned yet, something he could build that would make the waiting stop.

Neither Emma nor Jack was failing. But neither felt like they were moving forward.

Emma was starting to question what success actually looked like here.

Jack was starting to wonder if he had already fallen behind.

And neither of them knew that they were about to meet someone who would challenge what they thought they knew—and shift their entire paradigm.

PART 2

GETTING UNSTUCK

Letting go of old patterns, embracing imperfect action, building momentum.

CHAPTER 3

YOU'RE PLAYING THE WRONG GAME

It started with a question, not a motivational poster, not a lecture. Just a quiet, well-timed question that stuck at an alumni event that Emma and Jack attended.

Ram had been invited to speak at an alumni event for recent grads, lukewarm coffee, and too many folding chairs. Jack almost didn't show. Emma didn't plan to stay long. But something about the speaker's bio sparked her curiosity: MIT graduate, entrepreneur, author, coach. And, he had a GenZ daughter who'd recently graduated.

Ram didn't launch into a speech. He told many stories, including a short story about a time he thought he had it all figured out, until life punched him in the face. He then asked:

"How many of you feel like you've done everything right and still aren't getting the results you expected?"

A few hands went up. Emma's didn't, but her eyes did. Jack kept his hands in his lap, but inside, the question landed.

Ram smiled, not the polished keynote kind, but like someone who'd been there too.

"You're not alone," he said. "You're just playing a new game by the old rules."

"There's a new kind of gap out there," Ram said. "Recent grads used to enter the job market with a clear edge—cheaper, fresh, eager. Now, that edge is fading. Some of the smartest graduates, on paper, are still getting stuck. Not because they aren't intelligent, but because they lack Smartness—the real-world capabilities to figure things out, create value, and adapt fast."

Ram added, 'I've coached MIT grads, Harvard MBAs, and McKinsey consultants. They all ran into the same wall—you don't need more credentials. You need Smartness."

Emma leaned forward. Jack finally looked up. Something shifted. Not because they were handed answers, but because someone had finally named the real problem.

This wasn't about being smart. It was about learning how to turn one's smarts, credentials and advantages into real-world results. Ram wasn't there to hand them a formula. He was there to challenge them to figure out how, with new tools, new thinking, and real action.

The old game was over. The real world was different. New graduates need to grab the new playbook and learn to play by the new rules.

He pointed out to the audience that, as college graduates, they were among only 7% of the world's population. An elite group already, irrespective of which school they graduated from. Their challenge, now, was to figure out how to leverage their intelligence, degree and other advantages to achieve their aspirations.

Emma – The Cost of Just Doing the Work

Emma wandered around waiting to talk to Ram. At the back of the room was a table where a few copies of his book were stacked. Curious, she picked up a copy of *How Smart People Can Become More Successful*. She noticed the testimonial by Dr. Marshall Goldsmith, the world's #1 Executive Coach that said, "If you've ever felt like your brain is working overtime but your results aren't matching your effort—this book is for you." Then, she saw another testimonial by Sean Brown, the career chair of the MIT Sloan Boston Alumni Association which said, "Intelligence is your engine. Smartness is the steering. Ram teaches you how to drive to impact much more effectively." She got herself a copy.

She then went and found Ram. She waited until a few others had drifted away, then approached him near the snack table."

"You looked like something I said got your attention," Ram said.

Emma half-laughed. "Yes, your question: 'How many of you feel like you've done everything right and still aren't getting the results you expected?'"

"New job?" he asked.

She nodded. "Sixth month. I think I'm doing okay. But I don't really know. It's been quiet." Ram raised an eyebrow. "Quiet like calm? Or quiet like no feedback?" Emma exhaled. "No feedback. No idea if I'm doing things right or wrong."

Ram nodded. "And how do you know if you're succeeding?" "I don't," she admitted. "I just… do the work. Hope it's enough."

She didn't say it out loud, but the question echoed harder than she expected. That morning, while half-watching the news, she'd seen a segment about companies skipping entry-level hiring. One exec had said something like, *"We don't need as many analysts—we've automated a lot of it."*

Emma had paused, coffee in hand. The anchor had mentioned AI doing first drafts of research memos, performance slides, even market recaps. She heard, "Five 22-year-olds with ChatGPT can do the work of 20 recent grads" and "Even law firms are leaning on AI for paralegal work."

She didn't catch all the details. But she felt it. That quiet tug of doubt that said, *What if smart isn't enough anymore?*

She graduated just a few months ago. Already, the ground felt like it was shifting under her feet. Smart wasn't safe. Degrees weren't guarantees. And "just doing the work" and "do what you're told" suddenly felt more fragile than ever.

Ram didn't offer advice, just said, "What's one action you've been avoiding?" Emma paused. "I've had an idea, but I've been waiting for the right moment."

"There is no right moment," Ram said. "Only the moment you act."

He paused for a beat. Then added, "You're not in school anymore. In the real world, waiting for permission is how smart people stay invisible. Don't wait to be picked. Start where you are. Move something forward."

Emma looked at him, half-hoping for more. "But how do you know if it's working?"

Ram paused, then nodded toward the book in her hand. "Let me give you an example from that. You know Roger Federer, right? One of the most iconic and successful tennis players ever."

She nodded.

"He won only 54% of the points he played in his career," Ram said. "Barely over half. But he won 80% of his matches. That small edge—just a few percentage points, consistently applied—turned him into a legend."

Emma raised an eyebrow. "So, it's not about dominating every moment or winning every time?"

"Nope," he said. "It's about winning enough of the right ones. In work, as in tennis, the people who learn to turn small edges into repeatable *success habits*—those are the ones who build great careers. The difference between successful and stuck isn't talent. It's the consistent application of *success habits*.

She nodded slowly, absorbing it.

Ram continued, "You're looking for confirmation. A signal that says, 'this matters.' But results usually lag. What you *do* every day—how you show up, how you follow through—that's what compounds. One percent better each week? That may not be noticeable now. But stretch that over ten years… you're in a different league."

Emma looked down at the book again. The subtitle hit differently now: *How Smart People Can Become More Successful.*

"I guess I've been waiting for someone to notice," she admitted.

"Noticing comes later," Ram said. "Build the edge now. Results follow behavior."

That night, she scrolled through old graduation photos: filtered smiles, cheers, her honors cords swinging in midair. It all looked golden. But she realized something now she hadn't known then—simple and profound.

*"Nostalgia is a dish best served old.
And the future wasn't back there."*

Jack – Now What?

Jack hadn't planned to talk to Ram. But after the event, Ram caught his eye and nodded—a silent invitation. Jack walked over to him, near a cluttered bulletin board full of QR codes and forgotten flyers. Ram kept it simple. "Tough week?"

Jack gave a tired laugh. "Is it that apparent? Yeah… still job searching."

"How's it going?" Ram asked. Jack shrugged. "Applied everywhere. Got nothing. I'm being ghosted like the women did back at school."

Ram didn't flinch. "So, what are you going to do differently?" Jack blinked. "I don't know. Keep trying, I guess."

"Trying is good. Acting with intention is better. What have you learned from the silence?" Jack didn't answer. Ram let the quiet stretch. "You're not here to prove you're ready," he said finally. "You have to make things happen. If they aren't happening, you need to figure out how to."

Something about that line hit. Jack didn't nod. But he didn't walk away either. He just said, "Okay. So, what now?"

Ram gestured toward the back of the room. "There's a stack of books near the door. I wrote one that might help you think differently so you can get unstuck."

Jack followed his gaze. *How Smart People Can Become More Successful.* No promises. No hype. Just a possible next step.

He glanced at the testimonials taped beside the stack. One read: "Ram Iyer's book delivers the tough love every smart professional needs but rarely receives. He shatters the myth that intelligence alone guarantees success and replaces it with actionable strategies anyone can use to move forward. This is the book I wish I'd had earlier in my career—it's practical, honest, and refreshingly direct. If you've ever felt stuck despite doing 'all the right things,' this book is your roadmap out." —Michael Vermillion, President, Chicago Booth Alumni Club of LA.

Another caught his eye: "If you've ever wondered why your intelligence and hard work haven't taken you further, this book explains why and provides a path to achieve greater success." —Larry Lifson, President, Kellogg Alumni Association of Chicago (West).

Jack nodded and muttered to himself, "Maybe this book will give me some answers."

CHAPTER 4

FROM SMART TO SMARTNESS

They had started to move, not with clarity, but with questions. What used to define them no longer seemed to matter: GPA, credentials and accolades. The simple pride of being a graduate was losing its shine, and nothing obvious had replaced it... yet.

Letting go of that identity was uncomfortable. But some changes only happen when you outgrow who you've been. Just like a silkworm struggles out of its cocoon to become a butterfly, Emma and Jack were beginning to shed their college skins. Not because they felt ready, but because staying the same no longer fit who they were becoming. But it's the only way forward. They now had wings and the whole world to explore.

This chapter isn't about failing. It's about shedding the identity you were recognized for in school, with one you need to build in the real world.

Emma – Breaking the Smart Girl Spell

Emma wasn't failing. Her performance reviews were fine. She hit deadlines, stayed organized, and didn't make waves. But none of it felt like traction. At school, being impressive meant results: grades, awards, offers. But here? She was just… competent. Professional. A reliable cog in the machine.

She had started to notice the dissonance. Her GPA, once a source of pride, now felt irrelevant. Her degree hung on her apartment wall. No one else cared. She kept it there out of pride, and to remember what it had taken to earn it. What mattered now wasn't what she knew, but what she could leverage it to produce desired outcomes.

The more she observed her colleagues, the more she realized something uncomfortable. The people getting recognition weren't always the smartest. They were the ones who spotted opportunities, navigated ambiguity, 'made things happen' and produced results, however messy the process. It wasn't polish that mattered—it was progress and achievement.

> *"In school, being smart meant knowing the answer. In the real world, Smartness means knowing what matters—and acting on it."*

At lunch one day, after one of her ideas was dismissed in a meeting, she finally admitted it to herself: *My identity has been built on being the smart one. But here, no one cares about my intelligence, credentials or where I went to school. They're watching to see what I actually do.*

It stung. But it also freed her. Maybe it wasn't about trying to prove her worth. Maybe it was time to experiment. To build it. To earn it.

She closed her laptop that night with one quiet thought: *I need to stop proving I'm smart and start learning how to succeed. I will earn my success.* She remembered a quote from Ram's book:

> *"Smart people often assume intelligence will lead them to the right answer. But the real challenge isn't the answer, it's knowing the right questions to ask."*

Jack – From Blame to Bold Action

Jack had spent weeks blaming everything and everybody he could: the market, the companies, his school, his major, his professors, his classmates and his résumé. Some of it seemed fair. But the longer the silence from prospective employers dragged on, the more he noticed the pattern—he was waiting. Waiting for someone to pick him. Waiting for feedback. Waiting for something to shift.

Ram's words echoed: "You have to make things happen."

So, he did something different. He reached out to a small local startup that hadn't posted any openings. He wrote a note—not asking for a job, but offering to help solve a problem he'd seen on their site. He didn't hear back for a week. Then they replied: "Let's talk."

The conversation wasn't magical. But it was movement. And something clicked.

Maybe it wasn't about having the perfect credentials. Having a job gave him meaning. He realized that too many new graduates reject opportunities to gain experience which directly addresses their biggest issue with employability—the need for experience. Maybe it was about building judgment by doing, testing, learning, and trying again.

Jack still felt unsure. But he wasn't stuck. He was starting to act. He didn't feel like a nobody anymore. He remembered reading this quote from Ram's book: "I hate being a nobody more than I hate trying and failing."

Emma was letting go of the safety of credentials. Jack was letting go of the comfort of blame. Neither of them had everything figured out. But both had started the harder work, redefining who they wanted to become, not just who they'd been.

Because identity doesn't come from what's on your résumé, and you're not stuck being who you were. It comes from how you show up when things get hard, and who you choose to become.

And that's when Smartness starts to take root... in both of them.

CHAPTER 5

FIRST STEPS AREN'T FLASHY OR CERTAIN

Success rarely begins with a breakthrough. It starts with something smaller: a risk taken, a comfort zone stretched, a first imperfect step. Not flashy. Not clean—but real.

Emma and Jack weren't building confidence yet. They were building motion. And that motion, although uneven and awkward, was what they needed. They didn't need to be certain. They needed to start.

Emma – Naming the Illusion

Ram invited Emma to grab lunch. Nothing formal, just in a quiet corner of the cafeteria, but her inner overthinker had kicked in hard. Did this mean something? Was it a performance review in disguise?

Emma almost said no. But she showed up. Tray in hand, posture stiff, eyes scanning for signals. Ram nodded toward an empty table. Emma gave her an update on her progress and expressed frustration at the slow progress.

"You're not alone in this," he said, after a few bites.

"I've seen a lot of smart new grads stall out in the first year. Those with elite degrees, honors and sharp résumés, but still stuck."

Emma didn't say anything. But something about that word, *stuck*, landed harder than she expected.

"Three people come to mind," Ram said.

"Jason, Lena, and Ravi. All brilliant. All three floundered for different reasons."

He gestured with his fork. "Jason had all the credentials: valedictorian, top internships, natural presenter. But he wouldn't act unless he was 100% sure. Always waited for permission. If things didn't go perfectly, he'd spiral. He refused to act because he couldn't handle failure."

Emma nodded. That sounded uncomfortably familiar.

"Lena was confident. Too confident sometimes. She'd push her ideas hard but wouldn't adjust. People stopped listening. She was poor at reading emotional cues. Many refused to work with her. She quickly became an island unto herself."

"And Ravi? The guy was a Harvard MBA. He could analyze anything. Brilliant mind. Wrote killer PowerPoint decks. But he never shipped anything. Always overanalyzed, improved, tweaked—but never delivered. He thought the quality of his insight should speak for itself. It didn't. In meetings, people stopped asking for his input. Not because he wasn't smart, but because he never moved things forward."

He leaned back, eyes steady. "See, it's not just people with bachelor's degrees. I've worked with several MBAs and even MIT PhDs who struggled because they never developed Smartness or learned how to use it. They had the Advantage Illusion. The universal key isn't more credentials—it's learning to apply who you are and what you've got… with Smartness."

Ram let it sink in. Then added, "They weren't broken. They just had the wrong idea of what makes someone successful *after* school."

Emma looked up. "Like what?"

"They all fell into what I call the *Advantage Illusion*," Ram said. "It's what happens when smart people assume their intelligence, credentials, and effort should automatically lead to success—because that's how it worked in school. Many smart students get As with very little effort."

Emma exhaled. The description of Ravi hit a little too close to home. Ravi had the shine. But no traction. And for the first time, she realized Smartness wasn't just for those who lacked elite backgrounds. It was for anyone who wanted to move forward—no matter how stacked their résumé looked.

"But out here," he said, "you have to earn it again, every single time, with your behaviors, actions and performance. And, succeeding in the real-world usually requires a lot more than just intelligence. You'll need a lot of Smartness. But it isn't a flip switch. It's something that only you test, refine, and apply repeatedly to create real, repeatable success acting, over and over again."

Ram continued, "Smartness isn't just a skill. It's a set of real-world capabilities—built from how you think, act, learn, adapt, relate, and follow through. It integrates your skills, but it's what makes them effective in real-life situations."

Emma nodded slowly. "So, I can't just do more. I have to do different."

Ram smiled. "Exactly. You're not here to prove you're smart. You're here to figure out how to use your smarts in different situations to produce the outcomes you want."

Emma frowned. "I keep waiting for someone to coach me. I thought that's what employers were supposed to do."

Ram didn't flinch. "A lot of companies used to think that way. But now? They're stretched. They want people who already know how to get traction. People who can build value without waiting for instructions."

He paused, then added, "They're not going to train you. They're looking for people who can train themselves, or come with a high level of developed Smartness they know how to use."

Ram leaned forward, and with his voice lower but clearer, said,

"Success isn't just a science. If it were, more people would already very successful. The real world doesn't reward formulas—it rewards judgment, timing, adaptability, execution, and achievement. That's where Smartness comes in. It's not just about knowing what to do. It's about knowing how, when, and why to do it—and then executing to achieve the desired outcome. That's an art. The good news is that you can learn it and develop it with practice."

Ram paused and continued, "Knowledge decays. Fast,"

Ram said. "You're not hired for what you know. You're hired for how fast you can learn what you don't know. And you've got to be someone who doesn't flinch when the learning gets ugly. Employers won't always say it—but that's what they're really looking for."

Jack – The Offer, and the Mirror

Jack had read the first three chapters of Ram's book twice. The tone was blunt and clear, but it made sense—more sense than anything he'd heard since graduating. He wasn't expecting to agree with it. But the part that hit him hardest was this: "You don't have to get it right to get it going." He had underlined it. Folded the corner of the page. Then reopened it the next day like he needed permission all over again.

That afternoon, he sent Ram a short message through the website printed on the back cover: "If you have 15 minutes, I'd love to ask one question." Ram replied that night. "Let's meet at Starbucks. 3:30 tomorrow."

They met near the front window with two black coffees, one tired grad, one sharp-eyed stranger who didn't waste time. Jack got right to it. "I've got an offer. Startup. Small team. Low pay. But real work. I don't know if it's the right move."

Ram didn't flinch. "What are you comparing it to?"

Jack hesitated. "I don't know… what I thought I'd have by now, I guess."

Ram nodded. "That's the trap. You're measuring the present against an idealized version of success. That's how smart people stall."

Then Ram pushed his coffee aside. "Let's flip it. Don't just ask if it's the right move—ask what the fastest path to staying stuck looks like."

Jack blinked. "You mean like… how to fail?"

"Exactly. If you wanted to guarantee frustration six months from now, what would you do?"

Jack half-smiled. "Overthink. Avoid deciding. Wait for something better."

Ram leaned back. "And?"

"Keep scrolling job boards. Complain. Maybe take another course."

Ram nodded. "You just mapped the failure path. Now you know where not to go. It's not about knowing the perfect answer. It's about avoiding the obvious traps. Action reveals what works. Smartness grows from that."

Jack didn't respond right away. He didn't need to. He walked out of Starbucks and accepted the offer that night. No fanfare. No hashtag. Just a job. And a start.

From Stillness to Action

Emma and Jack hadn't figured it all out. Far from it. Real change rarely begins with a master plan. It begins with the decision to stop standing still. Each of them had taken a first step. That gave them just enough clarity to keep going.

Humans are a lot like sharks. Sharks must keep moving to breathe, hunt, and survive. If they stop, they suffocate. People aren't so different. When we stop acting, we stop learning, growing, and progressing. We drift. We stall. We decay.

Imagine a life of inaction. Just drifting. Then stuck. Then decay.

The journey of a thousand miles begins with a single step. Emma had taken hers. So had Jack.

INTERLUDE
I've Seen This Before

I've coached Ivy League grads and startup founders. I've spoken to alumni from MIT, Stanford, Harvard, Wharton, HBS, Booth, Kellogg, Ross, IIT, and more. These are sharp people with elite credentials. But many of them, even years into their careers, were still struggling with real-world success.

And I've watched my own daughter, a high-achieving graduate, face some of the same questions you might be wrestling with right now.

All of them were intelligent. Most had drive. Many had additional advantages like networks, resources, and skills. But they hadn't been taught what actually creates real-world outcomes in the world after school.

What they were missing had a name: **Smartness**. All of them had some of it. They didn't call it Smartness, but it showed up everywhere. Most people, particularly the unsuccessful ones, didn't develop their Smartness or learn how to use it in real-world situations. All of us have picked up some level of Smartness over our lifetime. But, developing Smartness by chance and circumstance is not enough if you want to become an achiever—someone highly successful and well above average.

They knew how to analyze, prep, and plan. But they didn't know how to navigate ambiguity, influence decisions, follow through under pressure, or act with clarity when things were uncertain.

They struggled to communicate impact, build trust, and move from potential to performance. Not because they weren't capable, but because they were never trained to play the real game.

It's not just people with bachelor's degrees. I've personally worked with elite MBAs, MDs—even PhDs—who struggle because they never developed Smartness or learned how to use it. The universal key isn't more credentials—it's learning to apply who you are and what you've got… with Smartness.

That's why I wrote this book—for them. And for you.

You're not broken. You're not behind because of who you are. You're behind because no one ever taught you how to succeed in the world beyond the classroom. Schools don't teach this—although they often claim to, or try to. That's because professors live in textbooks and academic systems (caves) where Smartness isn't required. But outside those walls, it is essential.

This book helps you close that gap.

If you've made it this far, a part of you already knows something is missing. You don't need a pep talk. You need someone to walk with you, to help you unlearn what no longer serves you and build the Smartness capabilities essential not just for success, but maybe even survival in the real world.

So, when you meet Emma and Jack, you're not just meeting characters. You're meeting archetypes: people with similar patterns who exist in real-life. Their frustrations, insights, and breakthroughs are drawn from real Smartness data and real stories from thousands of real graduates from across the world.

You'll watch what happens when people stop trying to prove they're ready—and start becoming ready.

If you've ever asked:

- Why are others getting ahead faster, even with fewer credentials and abilities?
- Why doesn't anyone explain how to succeed in the actual world?
- Why isn't intelligence or effort enough anymore?

This book won't just give you answers.

It will give you something better: a new way to move forward.

PART 3

BREAKING OLD PATTERNS

Core Smartness capabilities—judgment, self-direction, adaptability, relationships.

CHAPTER 6

FROM NOISE TO PROGRESS

Emma and Jack had both taken first steps. Not clean. Not certain. But steps, nevertheless. And with actions came exposure to noise, doubt, and the friction of being new. It didn't take long for old habits to sneak back in: overpreparing, overthinking, collecting knowledge without applying it. There was comfort in staying busy, in reading more, in building plans. But progress? That was something else entirely. And Ram knew it.

Emma—The Input Trap

Emma had always been the one who "came prepared." That was her reputation in college for being sharp, structured and detailed. She had shined by being the most prepared person in the room.

So, when her manager asked for a rough proposal on a product test, she delivered a 30-slide deck. Clear logic. Forecast scenarios. Backup data in the appendix. The works. Halfway through the meeting, Ryan from Ops leaned back and asked, "Emma, what's the one sentence you want us to walk away with?"

She blinked. Then hesitated. "I just wanted to show the thinking."

Ram, sitting in on the meeting, watched her. Quietly, afterward, he asked, "What would've happened if you'd sent three bullet points instead?"

Emma looked at him, confused.

"It wouldn't have felt... enough."

"Enough for who?"

She didn't have an answer.

Ram didn't press. Just waited, then added, "Ever heard of Inversion Thinking?"

She shook her head.

"It's a strategy smart people use when they're stuck. Instead of asking, 'What should I do to succeed?' they ask, 'What would guarantee I fail?' Then they avoid that path."

Emma blinked. "So, like... do the opposite of the failure route?"

"Exactly. You're not stuck because you lack effort," Ram said. "You're stuck because you're doing things that *feel* productive but don't actually move the needle. That's how smart people stay stuck, by being busy on the wrong things."

The words landed. Emma didn't respond right away. That night, she went home and stared at the open tabs on her screen: job boards, a writing course, another half-read self-help book, three podcast episodes queued up. It all felt productive. But none of it moved her forward. Just... noise.

Ram's words circled back: "The world pushes you to consume more—more advice, more opinions, more hacks. They usually fuel more anxiety, not achievement. Progress comes from action."

She closed the tabs. All of them. And opened a blank doc. One idea. One paragraph. One clear next step. Her need for variety was fine in school but it was killing her performance at work.

Progress wasn't about being prepared. It was about being effective.

And that started by asking a smarter question, "What else should I do?" However, that just adds to the noise.

They should instead ask, "What am I doing that's keeping me stuck?"

Inversion Thinking. For example, instead of asking what more you should do, ask what you must stop doing.

It wasn't a formula. Just a shift.

From doing more to stop doing.

From more effort to the right and smarter effort.

From input overload to output focus.

From proving readiness to creating results.

Jack – Inverting the Mirror

Jack had started working. It wasn't glamorous, but it was real. Still, on tougher days, the old reflex came back: complain and blame. The job was too small. The team didn't get him. The role wasn't what he'd hoped.

Over coffee one afternoon, Ram asked him, "What if you stopped asking, 'What's holding me back?' and started asking, 'Why am I holding myself back from excelling in this job?'"

Jack didn't answer at first. Then he shrugged.

"I guess… I keep comparing. To where I thought I'd be, or should be. Who I thought I'd be."

Ram stirred his coffee slowly. "Comparison feels productive," he said, "but a lot of the time, it's just avoidance in disguise."

Jack looked up. "You're not really asking if the job is good enough for you,"

Ram continued. "You're avoiding the harder question: Why don't you want to do well in this job?"

Jack blinked.

Ram didn't fill the silence. He let it hang. Then added, "Sometimes we sabotage progress because succeeding here would mean letting go of that imagined future we're still clinging to."

Jack didn't say anything, but his jaw tightened.

Ram continued, "Ask yourself: Am I judging this role? Or am I avoiding the discomfort of fully showing up in it?"

"Let me show you something."

He pulled out a napkin and drew a tiny circle. "This is the problem you could solve this week, something real and useful." Then a big cloud around it. "This is all the noise: your doubts, other people's opinions, all the stories in your head."

Jack stared at it.

Ram leaned in. "You'll get better answers when you start asking better questions. Brutally honest ones that may give you uncomfortable answers. Ask yourself, 'Is my idealized notion of where I should be realistic?'"

That night, Jack made a list of what he'd actually accomplished that week. Just three small wins. And one big task he'd been avoiding—the kind that could've made a real impact. Reflecting on his conversation with Ram, it hit him: the problem wasn't the job. It was his mindset.

He didn't like what he saw. But it was his. And that made it powerful. He knew his Smartness was developing.

From Activity to Smart Progress

They weren't consuming anymore. They were confronting their paradigms of progress. Not with bravado, but with awareness. Emma wasn't hiding behind input. Jack wasn't hiding behind blame. Both were learning something deeper: you don't grow by knowing more. You grow by doing different. You become more successful by producing results that matter.

Smartness had nothing to do with collecting. It had everything to do with leveraging what you have in the current situation.

And they were starting to do just that.

CHAPTER 7

BREAKING THE VALIDATION ADDICTION

Emma and Jack weren't lost anymore. But they were still distracted. The noise was quieter now, but another force had taken its place: the hunger to be seen. Applauded. Validated. Remember that you get feedback and validation in school quite regularly.

They didn't call it that, of course. Emma rationalized regular feedback as being useful. Jack rationalized it as necessary to build his brand. But underneath the effort, both of them were chasing something they couldn't control: constantly needing other people's approval.

It had worked in school. Perform well, get rewarded. But the real world wasn't handing out gold stars every day or every week. The applause came slower and infrequently. Sometimes, not at all. And that's when they started asking harder questions, not about what others saw, but about how they were showing up. For real.

Emma – From Activity to Purposeful Action

Emma was tired. Not the "long-day" kind of tired, but the "what-am-I-even-doing" kind. She was checking every box, staying late, even picking up others' slack. But the recognition never came. No nod. No thank you. Just another email, another deadline. One afternoon by the coffee machine, she loudly muttered, "I do everything they ask. Stay late. Pick up the slack. And nobody even notices."

Ram, who had just walked in, poured himself a coffee and asked, "Is that what you want? To be noticed?"

Emma looked up, caught off guard. "What do you mean?"

He glanced at her, voice calm. "I mean, are you working for impact—or for approval?" That stopped her.

Ram didn't flinch. "You're not here to be validated. You're here to figure things out. Don't wait for someone else to confirm what you already sense is true."

The words hit deeper than she expected. Emma had been waiting—on feedback, recognition, a thumbs-up from someone in charge. But maybe that wait was what was keeping her from moving forward.

Ram continued:

> *"Validation feels good, but it's not a foundation. You can't build a career on someone else's applause."*

He didn't linger. Just walked off.

Emma stood there, stunned by the simplicity of it.

That night, she opened her laptop, stared at a blinking cursor, and asked herself one question: "What outcomes actually matter on my projects to my organization?" Not what would get her noticed. Not what would earn validation or applause. What would actually drive results?"

It was a simple question—but it stuck. Because underneath it was a deeper one: Why am I doing any of this?

In school, she had always known her "why": get the grades, graduate, land a job offer, make everyone proud. But now that why had vanished—and nothing had replaced it. She didn't have a new north star to aim for each day. She remembered Ram's words:

> *"Your 'why' has to be bigger than the applause."*

Emma didn't have a 'why'. She made a note to figure that out—this weekend, without any distractions. For once, she wasn't trying to impress. She was trying to make something matter. Emma used to believe she had a growth mindset. Now, a growth mindset felt like fear dressed up as optimism.

The shift was small. But she embraced it.

Jack – From Sizzle to Steak

Jack had already bought the book after Ram's alumni talk, mostly out of curiosity. But now, frustrated and spinning, he finally cracked it open—unlike a majority of people who never read most of the books they purchase. One of the endorsements had stuck with him: *"Intelligence is your engine. Smartness is your steering."* At the time, he hadn't known what it meant. He did now.

He wasn't stuck because he wasn't smart. He was stuck because he was trying to look smart. Every move was calculated for perception, how he appeared online, how he phrased things in meetings, how fast he responded in Slack. But nothing was sticking. Because while he looked the part, he hadn't built the parts that mattered. His was unsure about his self-competence.

Reading the chapter on Self-Competence Views in Ram's book, he saw himself in every line. He had quietly doubted his value in this job, even while pretending to be confident. That insecurity had become a performance: confident on the outside, cautious on the inside. He had been sold the idea of "fake it till you make it." But the more he faked it, the hollower he felt.

A few pages later, the Outward Confidence chapter hit even harder. "When your confidence is performative, not grounded, it fractures under pressure." That was him. Overcompensating. Avoiding feedback. Worrying too much about how he came across.

He paused when he reached the chapter on how he was presenting himself. It wasn't about being slick. It was about being effective. Useful. Clear. He wasn't doing any of those. He was selling the idea of being capable, instead of becoming capable.

He sat back and realized that he had built the sizzle but hadn't seasoned the steak. He looked polished, but he hadn't developed the capabilities or competence to back it up. He felt like a fake.

So that night, he made a new kind of list. Not his to-dos, not his wins, but the habits that were quietly holding him back. The chasing. The posturing. The looking good for looking-good-sake. The fear of looking less than sharp. He didn't love what he saw. But it was his. And now that he could name it, he could change it.

From Applause to Impact

School and college had gotten him to constantly chase approval. But real growth? That comes from chasing impact. Emma was learning to stop performing for applause. Jack was learning to stop posturing for visibility. Both were learning to act, not for praise, but for purpose.

Applause fades. But Smartness, the kind built from honest self-awareness, ownership, and real output, is the stuff that compounds.

And both were developing their Smartness.

CHAPTER 8

SMARTNESS IS USED EVERY DAY AND EVERYWHERE

By now, Emma and Jack had both stopped waiting to be rescued. They weren't stuck, but they weren't exactly moving with purpose either. What they needed wasn't more motivation. It was clarity. Something to help them understand why they kept stalling out. Why intelligence alone wasn't cutting it. What they found next didn't come from a pep talk or a YouTube video. It came from seeing the same truth from a dozen angles—until it finally clicked.

Emma – Seeing It Clearly

Emma kept replaying what Ram had said to her by the coffee machine just a few days earlier: *"Are you working for impact—or for approval?"* It wasn't loud. It wasn't dramatic. But it stuck—the kind of line that made other thoughts feel noisy by comparison.

The words replayed in her head as she sat in her apartment that Saturday, wrapped in a hoodie, a coffee cooling beside her.

A few days earlier, Ram had mentioned his book and said, "If you're serious about impact, start there. See what sticks."

She had bought the book weeks ago—after their first conversation. It had been sitting on her shelf since, unopened, waiting for a moment when she was actually ready to read what it had to say.

She peeled it open. No highlighters this time. Just her, the book, and a quiet question she couldn't shake: *What does impact even look like?* She flipped through the opening chapters, letting her eyes scan until a bold line caught her attention:

"Intelligence is just a tool, like a hammer. Don't confuse it with the hand that wields it."

She froze. That was it. A degree is just a tool. Smartness is the hand that swings it. For the first time, Smartness didn't feel like some abstract concept. It felt like something she'd seen—but never named.

Maya, her coworker, never had the flashiest ideas but always knew how to get a meeting back on track. Rick, the intern, got a VP to adopt his slide—not by being brilliant, but by asking the right question at the right moment. *That's Smartness,* she thought. *Not knowing more. Using what you know better.*

Here's the updated section of **Chapter 8**, revised to match the **final, unchangeable quotes from the main book**, while preserving your original narrative structure and tone:

The next section made her smile:

"In poker, the best hand doesn't always win. The smartest player does."

"In chess, everyone starts with the same board. Smartness is how you play under pressure."

She remembered that offsite when the strategy was clear—but it fell apart in the room. Except for Nate. He read the room, shifted the tone, and salvaged the meeting. Smartness wasn't the plan. It was how Nate adapted when the plan wobbled.

Then came a line that hit closer to home:

"The strongest player doesn't always win. The one with better timing, awareness, and adaptability does. That's Smartness."

In school, Emma had always taken the shot. Always. Raised her hand. Volunteered. Did extra work for extra credit. But in the real world, taking every shot didn't help. Sometimes, Smartness meant letting the play develop. It meant waiting, watching, choosing, or passing the ball to an open player.

"Coaches pick players not for raw skill—but for Smartness under pressure."

She underlined that one twice.

The business section cut deeper:

"Smartness turns meetings into influence. It turns insight into traction."

"Smartness is what helps you fix the process when it breaks."

She thought about the last project she'd led. The process had broken, and she had panicked. Now she saw what was missing. Not more training. Not more authority. What she had needed was Smartness— the judgment to pause, ask for help, and redirect. And not go it alone.

"Smartness isn't a personality trait. It's a learnable set of capabilities."

Emma closed the book and looked around. Same apartment. Same coffee table. But something had shifted. She had seen Smartness applied in the world around her. Once you see Smartness, you can't unsee it. It was everywhere. In the office. In traffic. In conversations. It wasn't about being impressive. It was about being effective.

She flipped to the back of her notebook and wrote just one question: *Which one hit you?* Then she drew a line underneath it and answered: *Smartness is what helps me turn what I know into something useful. It's how I make it count.*

Jack – Reading Between the Lines

Meanwhile, Jack was sipping his coffee at the coffee shop one Saturday morning. He didn't want to listen to another podcast. He didn't want another carousel post telling him to optimize his mindset. What he wanted—what he needed—was something that worked when nothing was working.

He picked up Ram's book again—the one he'd started skimming last week but hadn't really absorbed yet. This time, he opened to a section he had bookmarked earlier, one he hadn't fully appreciated until now:

"Smartness is what keeps you in the room when things get messy."

That line stayed with him. It was like being quick on his feet. His week had been one long mess. A hand-off that never happened. A client call that veered off course. A meeting where he said all the right words and still walked out feeling irrelevant. He wasn't dumb. He was just… ineffective. And that was worse.

The next section laid it bare:

"Smart people don't fail for lack of knowledge. They fail when they can't turn knowledge into effective action. That's where Smartness comes in."

Jack paused. That's what it felt like. Like being smart had gotten him into the conversation—but not through it. He was showing up with answers. But no one was asking the questions he'd prepared for. As he read on, a pattern emerged. Metaphors, everywhere. Sports. Business. Poker. Chess. It felt like Ram was making the same point from twenty different angles, perhaps intentionally:

"Smartness is knowing when to strike, when to slow down, when to change the play, and when to do nothing."

Jack thought back to a team meeting earlier that week. His manager had paused mid-sentence, clearly looking for someone to speak up. Jack had a great point to make — sharp, insightful, and right on topic — but he hesitated. He wasn't sure it was the right moment. By the time he gathered the courage, someone else jumped in with a similar point. The team nodded. The conversation moved on.

Jack realized later: his insight wasn't the problem. His timing was. He hadn't read the moment — and missed his chance to lead.

He shut the book. Sat back. Let the truth sink in. You can't win on IQ alone. Not anymore. Not in the real world.

Smartness wasn't about being the fastest brain in the room. It was about being the one who could move things forward when the situation changes.

He opened his notes app and typed: *"Smartness is what turns your knowledge into traction. I need to get better at knowing when to speak up."*

From Ideas to Action

For both Emma and Jack, the metaphors landed differently—but the effect was the same. Smartness wasn't a new idea. It was a new lens. They'd seen pieces of it before. In others. In themselves. Now, with names, patterns and stories, it became usable. They weren't just reading a book. They were seeing capabilities they could build, and use, to be more effective in life.

And for the first time, it felt like he could play the game.

CHAPTER 9

SHIFTING FROM WHO YOU WERE TO WHO YOU NEED TO BE

The applause hadn't vanished—it had just gotten quieter. Subtler. Less predictable. And that silence was forcing Emma and Jack to confront something deeper than visibility: identity. Not their school identities, but ones that actually delivered results in the real world. The gap was becoming clear. What had once earned them praise was now getting in their way.

Emma – From Graduate to Worldly Grit

Emma sat alone in the conference room, half-scribbled notes in front of her, the door still slightly ajar after everyone else had filed out. She had said what she needed to say, shared her update, nodded through the feedback, and smiled in all the right places. But something wasn't clicking. Not with her colleagues. Not with herself. She didn't feel like a contributor. She felt like someone pretending to be one.

Earlier that week, her manager had gently pulled her aside: "Emma, we know you're smart. That's clear. But I need you to start anticipating what people need. For that, you need to think beyond the task."

It hit her like a light tap and a deep bruise at once. She nodded and said, OKAY. But inside, she was rattled. What did that even mean? She was smart. Wasn't that enough?

She'd worked hard for her degree. Graduating felt like proof that she'd made it. That she was capable. Smart. Ready. But here, in this world of vague expectations and moving targets, that identity didn't seem to matter much. She kept thinking, *I'm a college graduate. I should be able to do this.* But the truth was harder to admit: the job wasn't asking her to prove she was a graduate—it was asking her to figure out who she needed to become. And that was exhausting.

She brought it up with Ram over coffee that week. He listened, then leaned in gently and said:

"Sometimes the hardest part of growing up is letting go of who you used to be."

Emma nodded, slowly.

Ram nodded, then paused. "You've been loyal to your past. To the student version of you. To what worked before. But at some point, growth requires a shift."

> *"For many people, it's often easier to glow in the accomplishments of the past than to look forward to building your future."*

Emma didn't respond right away. But something in her posture shifted. He wasn't asking her to disown her history—just to stop clinging to it as the only way forward. She wasn't just listening now, but taking it in.

Ram continued, "That's where Smartness becomes a huge advantage. It's a capability that enables you to succeed in the present and the future, even when the next step feels uncertain."

"You've gone as far as your current approach will take you," Ram said. "To go further, you need to start using what you have more effectively."

Emma blinked. "What do you mean?"

"You've been holding on to the idea that being a graduate means you're smart," he said. "And because you've been told you're smart for so long, it's easy to assume that should automatically translate to success. That the degree proves you've arrived. Remember the *Advantage Illusion* I told you about? But the real world doesn't value that as much you do. "In school, being smart was your shield. In the real world, leaning on it too much could mask how unready you may be."

She didn't reply, but something about that felt uncomfortably true. She remembered reading about the 'Advantage Illusion' in Ram's book.

"In school, being smart was the game," Ram continued. "You got rewarded for it. You built your confidence around it. Many people embrace 'smart' as their identity. But success in the real world depends on your ability to understand situations and adapt. Being 'smart' helps but is not enough. You must ask: 'What does this situation require?'"

He paused, letting it land.

"Smartness helps you do that. It gives you the capabilities to shift how you show up. It's what allows you to take on different roles, depending on what the moment demands. One day you're the quiet observer. The next day, you're the one leading the room. That's not faking it, but being context-aware, role-flexible, and outcome-focused. That's

Smartness. Many smart people struggle because they try to succeed by being the same version of themselves everywhere, by tightly holding on to singular identities like, "I'm smart." But real success? That comes when you let go of trying to be smart all the time, and start focusing on being effective in any given situation." Ram paused, and continued,

> *"Intelligence is just a tool, like a hammer. Don't confuse it with the hand that wields it."*

Emma sat back in her chair, staring at the tabletop. She'd never thought of it that way. Maybe that was the shift she needed—not to prove she was smart, but to learn how to adapt to the moment. To stop clinging to the idea of who she thought she was, and start showing up as who the situation needed her to be.

She didn't feel ready. But for the first time, she knew what to start unlearning, and what she needed to work toward.

Jack – From Performer to Practitioner

For Jack, the shift came more slowly. It wasn't one meeting or moment, but a steady erosion. A quiet discomfort that followed him into every project. He'd started to notice how often he froze when expectations weren't clearly defined, how much energy he wasted trying to sound impressive instead of being useful.

He kept thinking the problem was external: unclear direction, bad culture, lack of mentorship. But eventually, he found himself staring at a different kind of question: What if the real issue was how he was showing up?

That question stayed with him. He opened the Smartness book again, this time reading deeper into the chapters on Self-Competence Views and Outward Confidence. The words stung.

"When your confidence is performative, not grounded, it fractures under pressure."

He saw the double life he was leading: sharp language in meetings, vague anxiety behind the scenes. The endless job title comparisons on LinkedIn. The subtle flexes on his résumé. The need to be seen as capable before he actually felt it.

But the chapter that stopped him cold was the one on self-presentation. It wasn't about polish. It was about alignment. Effectiveness. Utility.

"The more you try to look capable, the less you're able to become capable."

That line cracked something open. He realized he'd been so focused on being impressive that he'd neglected being impactful. So, that night, Jack wrote down a new kind of list. Not his achievements. Not even his goals. Just the habits that were holding him back.

Overcompensating. Overthinking. Avoiding feedback. Needing to look sharp instead of doing the work to become sharp.

He didn't like what he saw. But now he couldn't unsee it. And that made change possible.

Intelligence Is Not Identity

They had started to see that what school had rewarded wasn't always what life demanded. Emma was no longer clinging to the idea that her degree defined her. Jack was finally questioning the performance he'd been living. Both were letting go of the "smart" identity that had once given them pride.

They weren't more intelligent. Just smarter about how to use what they had. Intelligence, credentials, and strengths are all advantages. They are just like tools. And tools only matter if you know when and how to use them. That tool is Smartness.

A lion cub is born with hunting instincts, but not the skills. Even the strongest lion will starve without learning to hunt. You were born with intelligence and may have other advantages too. But just like the cub must grow from potential to capable, so must you.

That's the transformation both Emma and Jack had begun.

CHAPTER 10

DEALING WITH AMBIGUITY

Emma and Jack had begun to shed their student skins, but the real world wasn't offering neat rubrics or setting clear expectations. School had trained them to follow instructions, to check boxes, to hit clear targets. But work was different. There were no syllabi. No weekly grades. Just murky assignments, shifting priorities, and a silent scoreboard only the experienced folks seemed to understand. Ambiguity wasn't the exception here. Personal initiative was essential to find out what was expected, how the movers and shakers were, and what really mattered. It was the norm.

Emma – Navigating Without Directions

Emma opened her inbox to a message marked "High Priority." Her manager had asked her to explore a new partner integration. No template. No checklist. Just: "See what's possible and outline a rough approach."

She read it again and again. The task was vague. The goal unclear. And no one had told her what success looked like. After drafting and deleting three emails, she finally walked over to her colleague Nate.

"Hey," she said, trying to keep her voice casual. "Have you ever worked on a partner integration before?" Nate shrugged. "A few. But they're all different. You kind of have to just dive in and figure it out. Start, even if it's messy, and clean it up as you go along."

That phrase stayed with her. *Start messy*. It felt wrong. But maybe it was time to stop looking for the perfect plan and a perfect start. Instead, just begin. That night, she sketched out a one-page brief on what she knew, what she didn't, her initial take on what mattered, and how she could start.

The next morning, she sent it in. Her manager replied two hours later: "Great starting point. Let's iterate from here." Emma stared at the screen, surprised. Not by the feedback, but by how much lighter she felt. The task hadn't gotten clearer. But she had. Because she had taken the first step. Because sometimes, action elicits direction and makes ambiguity manageable.

Jack – Floundering Without Directions

Jack had always thrived on structure. Give him a checklist, a defined problem, a rubric and he'd crush it. But his new role didn't work like that. The instructions were vague. The outcomes blurry. His manager often said things like, "Let's see what you come up with." He hated that.

For weeks, Jack waited for clarity, for instruction, for something to react to. But nothing came. The silence started to echo. Frustration turned into doubt. Maybe he wasn't as sharp as he thought.

During a check-in, Ram didn't offer a solution. He asked a question:

"What do you think this job actually requires of you?"

Jack paused.

"I guess… figuring it out?"

Ram nodded.

"Exactly. Not waiting. Not asking for a rulebook. Learning to shape, adapt and drive to the outcome yourself."

Jack felt his resistance soften. For the first time, he realized that ambiguity wasn't the obstacle. His expectation for clarity was.

That night, Jack listed the three projects on his plate and wrote one bold next step for each. They weren't perfect, but forward. One small risk at a time. He was learning to use the strategy of making small bets. His confidence didn't leap, but something steadier did: a sense of ownership. And that changed everything.

From Rule-Followers to Results Achievers

School had curved life into neat lines. The real world doesn't. It deals in jagged edges, shifting rules, and blurry goals.

Emma had stopped fearing uncertainty. Jack had stopped waiting for instructions. Both were learning to create the clarity they once expected would be handed to them. They now know that in the real world, no one hands you the rubric. You build it yourself.

And Smartness? That's what lets you act in the face of ambiguity—with imperfect data, evolving goals, and your best judgment as the compass.

CHAPTER 11

USING YOUR LEARNING ADVANTAGE

School had made learning feel linear: listen, study, get tested, repeat. The pattern was predictable, the stakes low, and feedback structured. Many of the courses you took weren't connected—and it was up to you to integrate them in the real world.

Now that Emma and Jack were in the real-world, they had done a lot of things. Here, learning wasn't about getting it right the first time. It came from missteps, adjustments, doing, failing, learning, and doing again. This was the new loop. Messier, yes, but also far more powerful. Along the way, you also need to integrate different things.

Emma – From Reaction to Reflection

Emma sat stiffly as the team meeting ended. Some teammates had pointed out communication gaps, missed handoffs. Emma found herself explaining and justifying, trying to make sure they understood her point of view.

As the room cleared, Ram noticed her lingering, gathering her things slowly. He hadn't been in the meeting, but the frustration showed. "Tough one?" he asked.

Emma gave a half-shrug.

"I thought I was doing fine. I guess I got defensive."

Ram nodded.

"It happens. But Smartness isn't about defending your work. It's about seeing what actually happened and adjusting faster next time."

Emma stayed silent, then nodded slowly.

"You're not judged by how perfect you look," Ram added. "You're judged by how quickly you learn and improve."

She didn't love hearing it. But it didn't feel like criticism. It felt like challenge. And that made her want to do better.

She paused, still holding her laptop.

"I'm not sure this will work—this whole way of showing up—but I'm done waiting for certainty."

Ram smiled.

"Smartness doesn't start with knowing. It starts with trying—and sharpening your judgment with what you learn from what happens."

It wasn't a big moment. But it shifted something.

A few days later, her manager asked for a volunteer to lead an internal debrief on the last project: what worked, what didn't, what to improve. There was no formal credit. Just a quiet opportunity.

Emma raised her hand.

This time, she approached it differently. She didn't try to impress. She tried to learn. She started with simple questions. She framed the conversation around insight, not blame. And when she summarized her notes, she didn't just recap, she recommended. Her manager responded the next morning: "Great work. Share this with the directors."

It was a big win. Directors! Woohoo! Her modified approach was working.

Ram caught her by the coffee machine a few days later. "How did it go this time?"

Emma nodded. "I didn't just react. I reflected. I adjusted."

Ram smiled. "That's what Smartness looks like in real life."

Jack – From Misses to Little Wins

Jack had made three suggestions in his team Slack that week. All ignored. Not even a thumbs-up. He told himself people were just busy. But a quiet voice kept asking: *Was I off? Was I unclear? Was I adding value?*

He almost shut down. But something Ram had said weeks ago came back to him: *You don't grow from knowing. You grow from doing, failing, learning, fixing, and achieving. Sometimes, you have to find out by becoming Sherlock Holmes yourself.*

So, Jack didn't retreat. He revisited the messages. Looked for patterns. Then, instead of waiting for someone to tell him what was wrong, he asked a teammate: "Hey, was that idea off base? Be honest. I want to get sharper."

The teammate replied: "Honestly, the ideas were solid. But they got buried in too much text. Lead with a quick summary so people actually read it. TL; DR is real. If it looks long, most people won't even start reading." It wasn't an insult. It was insight.

The next time Jack had an idea; he posted it with three bullet points and a headline. That one got responses. And action.

The feedback loop had started. Not from a textbook. But from testing, watching, adjusting. A loop of real-world learning. He just went through a loop of the *Achievement Cycle* from Ram's book.

Turning Effort into Edge

Learning doesn't stop when school ends. But it changes shape. Emma had learned to see feedback as fuel, not judgment. Jack had learned to chase clarity, not just cleverness.

They were building something school never taught them directly: the loop of performance-based growth. Assess. Act. Reflect. Adjust. Repeat. That was the *Achievement Cycle* from Ram's book.

They weren't just learning how to work, they were learning how to learn by doing. It sharpens your judgment through every cycle. That's how Smartness grows: not from knowing the right answer, but from applying, adjusting, and doing it better the next time. Over time, that loop sharpens your judgment and builds your capabilities. And those capabilities become your edge.

CHAPTER 12

JOINING THE TRIBE

Emma and Jack were no longer navigating alone. But they hadn't yet found the people who could help them accelerate. In college, communities had been built-in—clubs, dorms, labs, fraternities, sororities, lunch tables. In the real world, it was up to them. And Smartness, they were learning, didn't grow best in isolation. It grew fastest with others: mentors, peers, even challengers who called them forward.

Before graduation, most people moved through life surrounded by peers on the same schedule, chasing the same milestones. But in the real world, people are scattered across different phases of life. Some are climbing. Some are cruising. Some are coasting toward retirement. They have their own routines, circles, and priorities. Most aren't looking to make new friends unless you give them a reason.

That was the disconnect Emma hadn't fully named. She wasn't being excluded. She just wasn't useful to them yet. In the real world, no one owes you community. You have to earn your way in by showing up, listening well, and contributing value.

That's where Smartness matters. Because you don't earn trust by trying to fit in. You earn it by figuring out what people need and helping meet it. You give people reasons to include you, not just in the project, but in their thinking.

And over time, strangers become allies. Coworkers become collaborators. And the tribe you build will do more than support you. As Ram puts it, "Mentors provide perspective and help you think better. Your tribe is both fuel and friction: they'll back you up and call you out."

That's what Emma and Jack were about to discover.

Emma — From the Edges to Plugged In

Emma had always prided herself on being self-sufficient. In school, that had worked: deadlines, group projects, even job applications. She was used to going it alone, but here, her independence wasn't always an advantage.

She noticed the shift during a cross-functional planning session. She had done her homework, polished her slides, and laid out the logic, but the conversation went sideways fast. Someone flagged a last-minute compliance risk. Someone else questioned the assumptions. Her argument held, but it didn't land.

Afterwards, she found herself standing by the coffee machine when Priya from ops walked up.

"You prepped like a pro," Priya said. "But next time, loop in Gabe from finance early. And consider pulling Jamie from legal. He spots issues before they blow up."

Emma nodded, slightly embarrassed. "I didn't think they'd have time."

"They will, if you give them a reason. Everybody likes to be needed" Priya replied.

That was the moment it clicked. This wasn't college. People didn't engage because it was required. They engaged when it mattered to their work, when it made their job easier or the outcome stronger.

That week, Emma made a list: who had insight, who had influence, and who followed through. She also asked around. Not to be popular, but to find people who could help her make an impact.

But there was something else she hadn't seen clearly until now. It wasn't just who you involved, it was how you communicated. During that meeting, she had made solid points. But her delivery didn't land. She rushed. She over-explained. When Jamie jumped in with something simpler, everyone leaned in.

Later, Priya told her gently, "It's not about dumbing things down. It's about helping people see what matters—and why they should care."

Emma hadn't thought of presentation as part of Smartness. But now she saw it clearly: even the best ideas didn't stick if people couldn't follow or feel them.

Ram had said something like that once: "Smart people often get ignored not because of what they say, but how they say it."

That week, Emma started paying attention—not just to what she said in meetings, but how others responded. Where they went quiet. What made heads nod. When energy shifted. It was like discovering a second layer of communication she'd never been trained to read. She found an entire chapter in Ram's book on communication and presentation choices.

The next time a project came up, she looped in Jamie and Gabe for early input. They showed up. The presentation landed. Her manager said, "That's the kind of cross-functional thinking we need."

Later, she told Ram about it. He nodded. "You're starting to find your tribe. Not the loudest people, but the right ones who will help you progress and be more impactful."

Emma smiled. *Wait.* She was starting to think like someone who belonged here, not just someone trying to keep up. She wasn't just building a network. She was building allies, resources, and alignment. Slowly, she was learning how to go further together.

She remembered the quote from Ram's book: "The smartest people know when to do it alone and when doing it alone is the dumbest thing they can do." She was getting smarter.

Over time, Emma had also started noticing changes in her tribe – who she spoke with, who engaged, who was on a similar path, and who she socialized with. Texts to college friends went unanswered. Weekend plans with some old friends faded. The group chats that once felt like lifelines were now mostly silent.

Over coffee one afternoon, she brought it up to Ram. "It's weird," she said. "People I thought would be in my life forever... are just kind of gone."

Ram nodded. "How your tribe evolves is often a sign of your own growth."

"How many of your middle school friends stuck around in high school?"

She thought for a moment and replied, "Not many."

"And from high school to college?"

"Even fewer."

"And now, after college?"

She smiled faintly. "Okay, I see your point."

Ram continued, "Don't get stuck mourning the people who leave. It's not always a loss. It's often just change. The ones who don't like who you're becoming, or who don't suit you for who you're becoming, are the ones who will fade. The right ones will stay with you or find you, or you'll need to find them."

He paused, letting it land.

"If you're not seeking people who will stretch your thinking, challenge you, or grow with you, you're not really growing. You're just running in circles."

Emma looked out the window, thoughtful, and smilingly said, "I guess I'm ready to start building the life that fits who I'm becoming."

> *"How your tribe evolves is often a sign of your own growth."*

Jack — From the Shadows to the Light

Jack didn't think he needed a tribe. He thought he needed results. But results weren't coming. He was delivering decent work, hitting deadlines, but it wasn't building momentum. His name wasn't mentioned in team huddles. People weren't turning to him for input. He felt like he was on the edge of the room, even when he was sitting at the table.

Then came a moment. After a client call, Drew, a senior analyst, pulled him aside. "You're better when you stop trying to sound perfect," Drew said. "You've got good instincts. Use them."

It wasn't a long conversation. But it cracked something open.

That week, Jack started asking a few more questions. He stopped trying to have the perfect answer in every Slack thread. He invited another junior teammate to join him on a small research task. Then another. Bit by bit, people started looping him in earlier.

One afternoon, over coffee, Ram said, "Smartness isn't just about what you know. It's about who you build with. You don't have to be the star. You just have to make other people better while achieving your objectives."

Jack had always assumed good work would speak for itself. But lately, it felt like no one was listening.

Jack told Ram about a project he had worked on for over a month—conducting detailed analysis, creating clean recommendations and a polished presentation deck. But when the deck went to the client, his name wasn't on it. Over coffee, he told Ram, "I thought I did everything right."

Ram shook his head. "You did. But it's not just about delivering great work but about being part of the process people remember. Don't work in the background and just send analysis and decks. Inject yourself into the meetings. Be in the room where your work gets used. It's easier to advocate for your yourself early—before the work is out of your hands, and where it matters. And that means getting informally plugged in with the team—before the work becomes final."

A few days later, Ram expanded on that thought: "The real world isn't a pure meritocracy," he said. "It's a visibility-ocracy. Quiet excellence is valuable—but if no one sees it, they can't build on it, reward it, or learn from it. As Dr. Marshall Goldsmith writes in *The Earned Life*, credibility must be earned twice. First, by delivering real value—through competence, expertise, or impact. Second, by ensuring others recognize that value. Results alone aren't enough, smart people must communicate their contributions and value clearly and visibly."

Jack let it land. Maybe it wasn't about chasing applause. But maybe it wasn't about hiding either. His instinct had been to impress. But now, he focused on enabling. On contributing consistently and visibly, and letting that building credibility and trust.

The shift was quiet. But real. He was starting to build his tribe too. Not a fan club. A multiplier. And that changed everything.

From Lone Wolves to Contributors

Emma was building alliances, not just for support, but for insights. Jack was becoming a contributor, not just a performer. Neither of them had found a perfect stride yet. But they were well on their way.

Smart people build tribes. Smarter ones grow together.

Because, in the real world, no one hands you belonging. You earn it by building credibility and trust, sharing effort, and with the Smartness to stop going alone. Yes, you can walk alone. But you'll walk farther, faster, and with less pain if you learn to walk with others.

INTERLUDE

Certainty, Doubt, and the Real World

Certainty feels safe. Doubt feels dangerous. And in school, safety was rewarded.

You followed the rubric. You knew the formula. You chased the right answer. The whole system was built on clarity and certainty. If you studied enough, you could be sure. And if you were sure, you could succeed.

But the real world doesn't work that way.

In the real world, nothing is guaranteed. The rules change. The answers shift. The feedback is slow or nonexistent. And the path ahead? Often unclear.

Naturally, we seek certainty. As individuals, we crave it. As customers, we demand it—just look at how often companies offer "100% money-back guarantees" to earn our trust. But when we get too addicted to certainty, we start waiting for it before we move. We delay action. We avoid risk. We seek permission. We fear mistakes.

And staying there too long makes you dependent—on guarantees, on feedback, on perfect timing, and perhaps somebody else's validation.

But certainty never shows up when you need it most. And even when it does, it's already in the past. Nothing is certain until it's already happened. Similarly, doubt never exists in the past, only in the present.

The most successful people aren't the ones who had perfect plans. They're the ones who learned to move forward without certainty. They made thoughtful bets. They failed, learned, adjusted, and tried again.

That's how judgment gets built. That's how self-confidence is built. That's how real success is earned.

> *"The most successful people are the ones who know how to thrive between the world's certainties."*

This is why Smartness matters. The *Achievement Cycle*—Assess, Target, Act, Reflect—isn't just a tool for high performers. It's a cycle that lets you learn through action. Not reckless guessing, but thoughtful iteration. Progress and success come from what you do now and what you will do next—not from what you did in the past.

Reflect, learn and adapt. That's how you win more often than you lose. Not by having the right answers, but by developing your Smartness, and therefrom your judgment to make better decisions.

> *Certainty is useful when looking back. But it's a poor guide when looking forward.*

PART 4

BECOMING EFFECTIVE

Transition into ownership, action, and building a life of continuous loops and progress.

CHAPTER 13

FROM STUMBLE TO STRIDE

Emma and Jack had built some momentum. But no growth comes without some slips. In school, the rules were clearer: if you failed, you got a bad grade. You may get lucky and get graded on a curve. But in life, there's no extra credit for hiding missteps—and no curve to bail you out. The real measure is how quickly you learn—and recover—from your setbacks.

As you already know, everyone stumbles. Yes, every one. Smartness isn't about eliminating failures or stumbles—it's about recovering faster and better.

Emma – From Misstep to Momentum

Emma thought her project was on track. It had been humming along until the client review. Halfway through her presentation, a senior manager interrupted. The numbers were off. The insights didn't land. It wasn't what they needed. The meeting ended abruptly. Later, she and her boss were pulled into a closed-door discussion. The client pointed out wasted effort, missed context, and demanded a recovery plan.

Emma didn't even go home. She found herself walking to Ram's office instead. "I blew it," she said quietly, standing in his doorway.

Ram didn't rush to reassure her. He listened. Then said,

> *"Momentum isn't about never falling.*
> *It's about how quickly you move again,*
> *smarter, sharper, and stronger."*

He pulled up his book and pointed her to a page with highlighted text, "Every time you stumble, you get a new cycle: Assess. Target. Act. Reflect. Adjust. That's how Smartness is really built." It was in a chapter titled, "How Smart People Can Become More Successful."

Emma sat with that. She'd been too focused on the dashboard and the deck. She'd missed key voices—like Priya's suggestion to talk to a frontline team member. She hadn't dug deep enough. She hadn't solved the right problem.

She reread the team's notes—this time, without defensiveness. She identified the blind spots, the assumptions and the gaps.

The next morning, she emailed her manager: "I've been thinking about our presentation. We focused on patterns but missed causes. I'd like to take another pass with a smaller scope, tighter questions."

He replied within ten minutes. "Good idea. Let's talk."

This wasn't the win she wanted. But it was the lesson she needed. Smartness grows through cycles, not perfect scores.

Jack – From a Quiet Fall to Confidence

Jack's stumble wasn't catastrophic. But it was public and sharp. During a client Q&A, he fumbled a basic point. Tried to bluff through it. Got gently corrected by his manager. Not cruelly, but clearly in front of the entire team.

The rest of the meeting passed in a blur. Jack nodded, took notes, tried to seem unfazed. But inside, the old voice started whispering: *Maybe you're not cut out for this. Maybe you're in over your head.*

That evening, Jack sat with his laptop open but untouched. His mind kept replaying the moment. The mistake wasn't huge. But the feeling? It stuck. Not because he failed. But because he didn't know how to recover.

He pulled out his phone and texted Ram: "Fumbled in front of a client today. Could use 15 minutes today if you've got it."

Ram replied twenty minutes later. "Starbucks. 7 p.m."

They met at a quiet table by the window. Jack recapped the moment. The stumble. The spiral.

Ram didn't flinch. "Everyone falls. But Smartness isn't about appearing perfect. It's about recovering faster than your fear wants you to."

Jack didn't respond right away. But something shifted.

The next morning, he didn't rehearse comebacks or try to fake confidence. He focused on clarity. He sent follow-up notes from the meeting, rechecked client data, and asked one of the senior analysts for input. He wasn't doing any of it to impress. He was doing it to gain clarity.

Later that week, he recapped the incident in his notebook. What he missed. What he misunderstood. What he'd do differently. He was applying the *Achievement Cycle*—sharpening his judgment, Smartness, and preparing to do better next time. It wasn't about erasing the stumble. It was about turning it into a sharper stride.

Recovery Is the Real Win

Emma stumbled. Jack slipped. But neither stopped.

School punished failure and judged you. Life rewards recovery and results. And Smartness? That's what helps you cycle through a stumble—quickly. Not by hiding. Not by defending. But by assessing, acting, reflecting, adjusting.

That's how confidence is built. That's how careers grow.

You don't fail when you fall. You fail when you stop learning and adjusting. The reason is often ego.

CHAPTER 14

FROM LEARNER TO GUIDE

Growth doesn't stop when you find your footing. It deepens when you help someone else find theirs. And if leadership is in your path, lifting others is where it truly begins.

And for Emma and Jack, the next level of learning came when they least expected it. Not as feedback, but as guidance. Not by being taught, but by trying to teach. Not as experts, but from right where they were. Because nothing sharpens your own thinking like helping someone else figure it out.

Emma – From Coaching Comes Confidence

Emma was still recovering from the sting of the client stumble when her boss stopped by her desk one afternoon. "Emma, Sofia is a new employee. She could use someone to show her the ropes. Would you mind spending some time with her?" Emma blinked. She hadn't expected that. *She still felt like she was figuring it out*, but she accepted.

Later that day, she brought it up with Ram. "I don't feel qualified," she admitted.

Ram looked at her, calm. "Emma, sometimes you have to trust other people's read on you, especially when their expectations stretch your own."

She paused, then nodded slowly.

He added… "It's not about having all the answers. It's about helping Sofia find hers. And in doing that, you'll see how far you've come."

Emma dropped Sofia an email and set up lunch. And as they talked, she heard her own early doubts echoed back at her. The questions. The hesitations. It was like listening to a younger version of herself.

As the days passed, Emma found herself explaining things she hadn't realized she now understood clearly. Context she could now give. Pitfalls she could help Sofia avoid. By helping someone else make sense of the work, her own Smartness develop further.

A week later, she slid a book across Sofia's desk with a quiet smile and said, "This helped me when I was getting my footing. Might help you too."

It was the same book Ram had handed her: *How Smart People Can Become More Successful.*

Smartness wasn't just about performing. It was also about passing it forward. Emma was learning that coaching was a mirror which showed how much she'd really grown.

Jack – Experience Maketh a Guide

Jack's coaching moment came with less ceremony, but no less impact. His college roommate Nate called one night, frustrated and stuck. No interviews. No responses. "I don't think I've got what it takes," Nate muttered.

Jack listened. Then remembered something Ram once told him: "You don't need to be an expert to help someone. Just one step ahead." So, he walked Nate through what had helped him. How to write sharper outreach emails. How to show up to informational calls. How to stop sending the same résumé into the void and start solving real problems for real companies. They talked for over an hour. Jack didn't sugarcoat things, but didn't hold back either. When they hung up, Nate sounded lighter.

Jack put down the phone and realized something: he had never said these lessons out loud before. But sharing them with Nate helped reinforce them in his own mind. He didn't just remember what he'd done, he also understood why they had worked.

He still didn't feel like a mentor. But he didn't feel lost either.

Helping Sharpens You

Helping someone else doesn't just benefit them. It helps you see your own journey more clearly.

Emma had begun seeing her growth through Sofia's eyes. Jack had turned scattered lessons into clarity. Both were now operating from something deeper than experience. They were building influence without authority, and growing the kind of wisdom that sticks.

Because mastery isn't just what you know. It's also what you can teach. And Smartness grows even faster when it's shared.

Curious where you stand with your Smartness?

You can take the *Smartness Assessment*—normally a $198 value—**for free** at www.MySmartness.com/Assessments. It's been taken by thousands of graduates from across the world – from California to Australia.

Use discount code: ***NewGradBook*** at checkout. You'll get an email with your *Smartness Assessment Report* on how you stack up on the 21 Smartness Factors within minutes.

CHAPTER 15

DISCOVER WHAT FITS

You don't need clarity to start. You need to start to gain clarity.
Emma didn't know what her dream job was. Jack didn't either. Not exactly. But they were learning that was okay. Most people don't "figure it out" before they start. They test. They try. They learn from doing, not from waiting.

In school, it had felt like you needed a plan. A major. A path. But out here? There were no fixed tracks. Only experiments.

Look around you. Many mid- and late-career people aren't in jobs that have anything to do with their college majors. Many have had multiple careers. That's how it works in the real world—nobody's got it all figured out. That's the point.

Emma — Questioning the Fit

Emma had something bugging her. She was clear about her role and liked what she was doing. But something about it felt smaller than it should. Like she was playing inside the lines of someone else's sketch.

That weekend, over coffee with Anita from marketing, Emma shared the feeling. "I'm executing. I'm contributing. But I don't know if I care about what we're building."

Anita didn't flinch. "That's normal. You don't have to love everything you do. But if something's tugging at you, follow the thread. Volunteer for a different type of project. Shadow someone. Join a cross-functional project."

Anita went on, "One of the best things I've found is to have an informational interview. Contact somebody who does the kind of work you think you may want to do. Tell them upfront that you are just exploring that as a career. Most people are very happy to talk about what they do. If you like what you hear, explore further."

Emma nodded slowly. It wasn't about quitting or jumping ship. It was about running small experiments. Looking for places where her curiosity could breathe. She decided to start by setting up lunch meetings with people in other departments.

That night, she made a list of roles she'd heard that she'd like to explore. Not because she was ready to switch, but because she wanted to test her own hypothesis to see what could fit. She messaged two people the next morning.

Jack — The Hypothesis Shift

Jack stirred his coffee, staring out the window of Starbucks. The *Smartness Assessment* had given him clarity on what was helping and what was hurting. But one question kept tugging at him. *What do I actually want to do?* He hadn't said it out loud until now. But it had been hovering for years, even before he started college.

Across the table, Ram let the silence linger. Then asked, "What's your hypothesis?"

Jack looked up and asked, "For what?"

"For the kind of work, you might thrive in. Not the job you think you should have. The kind of work that makes you feel alive, where your strengths could turn into results, and where you'd be excited to work and get better even on the hard days."

Jack leaned back. "I don't know."

"That's fine," Ram said. "Most people don't. The problem isn't not knowing. The problem is not testing."

Jack raised an eyebrow.

Ram went on. "In school, they made you declare a major. In many cases, you could change your major if you don't like it. In life, you need a hypothesis about the career you want. A working theory. Then you test it. I've had multiple careers. What I do now has nothing to do with what I studied in college."

Jack was quiet.

"You don't need to find your perfect career on the first try," Ram said. "You need a hypothesis—an idea about the kind of work that could fit you, excite you, or grow with you."

Jack jotted something in his notebook, then looked up. "So… I don't need to know for sure. I need to explore careers I find interesting."

Ram smiled. "Exactly."

Discovery Through Exploration

In school, you were graded on answers. In life, you're rewarded for exploration and outcomes.

The goal isn't certainty; it's to gain clarity—figuring out what fits by ruling out what doesn't.

It's a lot like dating. You go out with someone you like, until you realize they're not a fit. Then you keep dating until you find someone who is.

Apply that same thinking to your career—you're 'dating' different career options until you find 'the one' that fits you.

Career aspirations aren't declared. They're discovered—by exploring. By testing what fits, what doesn't, and what energizes you enough to keep going when it's hard. And Smartness? It's what helps you stay curious, open, and honest through it all, learning from successes and failures, so you can keep exploring with intention, even when the path isn't obvious.

CHAPTER 16

THE REAL SCORECARD

College taught them how to graduate. Now it's time to learn how to succeed. But first, they need a plan.

The real world demands something different: Self-awareness. Clarity of aspirations. Knowledge. Reflection. A clear view of where they stood, not compared to others, but in relation to who they wanted to become. Smartness isn't something we're born with. It's not static or finite. Everybody needs to learn how to develop and use it. It is a set of buildable, trackable capabilities. Anybody can develop it at any age or stage in life. New graduates are particularly well equipped because they are experts: they know how to learn! But before they could grow it, they needed to see it. That starts with assessing where they stand now.

A week earlier, Ram had sent them each a link to the *Smartness Assessment*. Now, with their results in hand, Emma and Jack were about to learn something most smart people never do: where they truly stand and what to do about it.

Emma – From Blind Spots to Building Blocks

Emma had always considered herself self-aware. But reading her *Smartness Assessment* results left her unsettled. Out of the 21 Smartness

Factors, she had seven enablers, three disablers, and eleven mixed. The report didn't just show strengths, it showed contradictions.

She skimmed one line again: "Relational Adaptability—Mixed."

That stung. She prided herself on being easy to work with. But deep down, she knew the truth. When things got stressful, she tended to shut down or double down, either avoiding the issue or becoming controlling.

She met Ram that afternoon.

"I thought I'd come further," she said.

Ram didn't argue. "You have," he said. "But Smartness isn't about being flawless. I haven't seen anybody who has all 21 Smartness Factors as enablers. It's about recognizing where you are and where you tend to stumble, and making small shifts that move you forward."

Emma nodded. "So, the mixed ones… they're like blind spots?"

"They're more like hinges," Ram replied. "They swing both ways. In the right setting, they support you. In the wrong one, they drag you." He paused. "The difference is your awareness and your response."

Emma looked down at the page. "So, if I focused on shifting my mixed ones…"

"You'd build more enablers," Ram finished. "You'd tip your system forward."

Later that week, Emma sat with the *Smartness Playbook* Ram had mentioned, flipping through exercises designed to convert insight into action. She wasn't trying to ace everything anymore. She was trying to grow by acting and using the *Achievement Cycle*. Not all at once. But with intent—one cycle at a time.

Ram had asked her to retake the *Smartness Assessment* every few months to evaluate progress. He had pointed out that Smartness evolves over time, and the report provides a snapshot view of one's Smartness.

She realized: this wasn't about being evaluated. It was a simple way to track her progress.

Jack – Counting What Counts

Jack sat across from Ram, flipping the *Smartness Assessment* printout. "I've got eight enablers, two disablers, and eleven mixed," he said. "So, I guess I'm doing okay."

Ram let the silence stretch. "Most people think success comes from their strengths," he said. "That's only part of the story. The real drag comes from the disablers, and even more so from the mixed factors. The ones you sometimes lean on—and sometimes trip over."

Jack looked up with his eyebrows raised.

"Mixed factors are tricky," Ram continued. "They work for you in some situations but against you in others. Like confidence in interviews, but freezing when the stakes rise. That confusion holds people back."

Jack frowned at the paper. "So, they're not bad… but they could be."

"Exactly. And here's the good news: mixed factors are pliable. You can shift them to enable your success more often… if you do the work."

Jack paused, then asked, "If I converted my eleven mixed into enablers, I'd have thirteen enablers. That would change the game for me, right?"

Ram nodded. "It certainly would. Most people never even take the *Smartness Assessment*. They float through life, busy but misaligned—mistaking constant activity for meaningful progress. It's more common than you think. They guess. Or worse, they assume their results are based on talent, intelligence, credentials or luck."

He continued, "Jack, you've taken the first step. You're already more self-aware than most people will ever be. Now it's about what you do with the insights."

"So, what do I do?" Jack asked.

"You leverage the enablers. You mitigate the disablers. And you work on those mixed ones until they tip the scale in your favor. That's how you build your Smartness Map."

Jack sat back. "What about everyone else? Where do they end up?"

"About 10% do the work and become more successful. Another 10% do nothing. The rest? They do a little here and there, usually when frustrated, but mostly drift."

Jack exhaled slowly.

"With the right Smartness," Ram said, "that middle 80% can go farther, faster, and with less friction. But they have to shift. Otherwise, they stay smart and stuck."

Jack folded the paper and tucked it into his notebook. Still no clever comeback. Just a quiet, determined nod.

Ram added, "From analyzing the data from thousands of graduates who took the Smartness Assessment, we found that 96% of the unsuccessful people know what to do but fail to act. 96%. Stuck in place because of inertia."

He went on, "The Smartness Playbook can help you build your personalized Smartness Development Map. Use it. Build your plan. Execute your plan using the *Achievement Cycle*. That's how real success is achieved."

The Real Scorecard

In school, grades measured their success. But now, Emma and Jack were learning that life doesn't hand out rubrics. It hands out results – success and failure. Smartness gave them a new kind of scorecard—one they built themselves, refined over time, and used to get better. You can constantly improve and use your Smartness, whatever your age or stage, all your life.

The world will always try to hand you its own metrics. But lasting success comes when you build your own and let it guide you toward who you're becoming.

CHAPTER 17

UNLEARNING THE SCHOOL RULES

Emma and Jack were making progress, on the outside. But on the inside, something quieter was unfolding. Not every belief they'd carried from school was serving them well. Some would have to be let go.

In school, the goal was to accumulate knowledge. In real life, it's about applying what you have and learning only what you truly need. Progress doesn't always come from gaining more; it often comes from unlearning what no longer serves you.

Old rules had shaped them for years: *Wait for feedback. Be thorough every time. Avoid mistakes at all costs.* Those rules worked in school. But now, they were slowing them down. If they didn't confront them, those habits wouldn't just hold them back, they'd become anchors.

Emma – From Praise-Seeker to Self-Believer

Emma had always taken pride in being "the reliable one." The one who stayed late, double-checked everything, smoothed over tensions. But lately, she had started noticing a pattern. Every time she received praise, she felt energized. Every time she didn't, she questioned her worth.

That wasn't confidence. That was addictive dependence.

One day, after a big presentation which elicited no standout feedback, Emma caught herself spiraling—checking email, refreshing Slack, rereading comments, searching for some signal that she was still being seen and recognized positively.

She paused, closed her laptop, and whispered to herself, *This can't be the game I keep playing.*

Ram's words from an earlier conversation drifted back: "If you only feel valuable when someone claps, then you're not building your own foundation."

Then she remembered something from the Smartness book:

> *"Bad habits come easy; good habits don't."*

and

> *"Doing the wrong things is often easier. Doing the right things repeatedly is sometimes hard—until they become automatic."*

She had spent years learning how to earn praise, and had gotten addicted to needing it. Now, she had to unlearn the constant need for it and rely on her self-worth.

Jack – From Polished to Proactive

Jack stared at the draft email, his cursor blinking. It was a simple question for his manager, but he kept second-guessing the tone. He was waiting at the Starbucks for Ram.

Ram walked up and asked, "What's happening, Jack?"

Jack sighed. "Just one email. I've rewritten it five times."

"In school," he said, "you check and recheck assignments to get a good grade. You aim for perfection—because the rules are clear, and the score matters."

Jack didn't look up.

"But life doesn't grade you like that," Ram continued.

> *"Timely action matters more than polishing every word."*

He paused, then added, "You need to get unschooled in many things that school trained you to do."

Jack hit SEND.

No speech. No drama. Just a quiet shift—and action.

From School Rules to Real-World Growth

Unlearning isn't dramatic. It's quiet. It's hard. It's essential. Emma had started letting go of her need for praise. Jack had started letting go of his fear of mistakes. Both were beginning to shift not just how they worked, but who they were becoming.

Because in life, you're not just rewarded for what you've learned. You're shaped by what you've had the courage to unlearn. Particularly as you enter your mid- and late-career, your disablers will pull you down much more than your enablers will pull you up.

CHAPTER 18

SMARTNESS: THE PLANNING BEGINS

A week later, Emma and Jack sat with their *Smartness Assessment* results in hand.

The report, unlike a grade or a score, had no pass/fail. There were enablers and disablers. Mixed traits. There's no set number of each that you must have or not have. It was a snapshot of how they operate at this point in time.

Emma had six enablers, three disablers, and twelve mixed. She stared at one of them: *Emotional Intelligence, mixed factor*.

It didn't surprise her. She often sought feedback, but struggled when it wasn't delivered gently. Her mind replayed moments she'd spent justifying her actions instead of listening. The assessment hadn't exposed a new flaw—it had confirmed one she already knew. She realized she wasn't just reacting to feedback, she was avoiding discomfort, and that was slowing her growth.

She met with Ram later that week. They sat on a bench outside the building, notebooks open.

"You're here to figure out how to leverage what can enable your greater success, and figure out how to mitigate what disables you." He continued, "You'll learn how to make the most of who you are, and what you have."

Emma nodded. "So, what do I focus on first?"

"Start with the mixed ones," he said. "They're the swing votes. Push them to the enabling side and things start improving quickly. Pick the mixed factors that you think are disabling you the most."

Emma circled three traits. Ram smiled. "Those are your development targets. You need to come up with a plan to make them more enabling and less disabling."

Across town, Jack met Ram at a coffee shop.

"I've got eight enablers, two disablers, and eleven mixed," he said. "So, I guess I'm doing okay."

Ram nodded. "That's a solid start. Now the real work begins."

He leaned forward. "Learn to leverage your enablers. Mitigate your disablers. Work on the mixed ones so they enable your success, more often."

"And remember," he added, "even small shifts—maybe just 1% improvements—compound over time. That's how Smartness works. You don't have to overhaul everything. You just need to keep nudging forward."

Jack listened, eyes narrowing as he processed it.

"Only about 10% of people who take the *Smartness Assessment* do the work and become more successful. Another 10% do nothing. The rest?

They dabble, often when they're frustrated, but mostly drift through life. They periodically act when they get bouts of inspiration or regret," Ram said.

Jack exhaled slowly.

"With improved Smartness," Ram added, "the middle 80% can become more successful. But if they don't shift, they stay smart… and stuck. In other words, a vast majority of people can achieve greater success."

Jack closed the notebook. No clever comeback. Just a quiet, determined nod—and the weight of what came next.

Customized Smartness Development

Emma and Jack weren't guessing anymore. They weren't hoping vague effort would turn into clear progress. They had development targets, and now it was time to build their Smartness with intention. They started working with the Smartness Playbook to build their personalized plan.

PART 5

BUILDING MOMENTUM

*Sustaining growth through continuous
learning, reflection, and application.*

CHAPTER 19

MEETING AT THE CROSSROADS

Developing Smartness was personal. But it didn't have to be solitary.

Emma and Jack had never met. Not until Ram invited them both for coffee one late Saturday afternoon. No agenda. No titles. Just two people figuring things out, and one quiet mentor who had seen their paths beginning to converge.

They sat across from each other at a small table in the corner of a quiet café, each with a notebook, a drink, and a mind full of questions. Ram stirred his tea slowly, letting the silence breathe before he spoke.

"You two are further along than most," he said. "You've started building Smartness, even if you didn't know to call it that."

Emma smiled faintly. "Still feels like guessing half the time."

Ram nodded. "That's how it works. Smartness isn't built in a classroom. It's built by taking action. You reflect. You adjust. You redo. You grow."

He looked at them both.

"A lion cub doesn't know how to hunt," he said. "Its mother doesn't just feed it, she demonstrates how to hunt. The cub learns by observing, mimicking, failing, and trying again—until it improves. Without those repetitions, it stays dependent, or it starves. Graduates are the same. If you don't build Smartness, learn from people who have, you will remain stuck."

He continued, "Reading helps. But Smartness develops through practice, constructive feedback, and the kind of tribe that grows with you."

Jack tapped his pen against the edge of the table.

"That's why peers matter," Ram continued. "You could go far alone—but farther with people who challenge you, point out your blind spots, and help you avoid traps."

Ram leaned in slightly.

"So don't just think of this as a meeting. Think of it as the beginning of a Smartness Circle. A peer alliance. Learning alongside someone else who gets it. Who's in the game with you. Someone you can compare notes with, and build alongside."

Jack gave a small nod. Emma jotted something down.

Ram smiled. "That's the trick. Smartness grows faster with others. You still have to do the work—but you don't have to do it alone. Sometimes, you just need someone to talk it through with. Someone who can challenge your thinking, push you to act, hold you accountable, or help you see what you missed, so you can keep improving."

Ram stood up, sipping his coffee.

"You don't need me for this part. You've got each other. You've got the tools. Now, build your Smartness by living it."

Without fanfare, Ram left them to it.

As they sat in silence, letting it all sink in, Jack recalled something else Ram had once said:

"Some of you may already be strong in certain aspects of Smartness and weaker in others. Don't let that turn into envy. Jealousy wants more for self and can push you forward. Envy, on the other hand, wants less for others—and drags everyone down."

From Solo Travelers to Smartness Allies

The conversation started with a few awkward pauses—misread signals, clumsy phrasing, and memories of early stumbles that still made them wince. But as they shared, something shifted. Emma talked about coaching Sofia. Jack mentioned helping Nate. They didn't trade titles or achievements. They traded Smartness Stories: hard-won lessons from real action, real reflection.

They realized they weren't just surviving anymore. They were building something sharper, stronger, and theirs. They weren't finished products. They were just getting started. And they weren't building alone anymore.

No declarations. No master plans. Just a new thread being tied between two paths. Quiet, but strong. And that's how they can become better.

CHAPTER 20

IT'S ON YOU NOW

About six weeks had passed since Emma and Jack first met. They weren't close, but something about their parallel paths kept pulling them into the same circles. Same project rooms. Same questions.

That Friday, they found themselves at the Starbucks again. Ram joined them at a small table in the corner, his coffee already in hand.

Emma flipped her laptop shut. Another online job panel and another hour of polished advice and some vague encouragement. She glanced at Jack, who was scrolling through a thread on certifications.

"You ever notice how all these experts say companies want problem-solvers, collaborators, people who take initiative… but no one teaches you how to become that?"

Jack didn't look up. "Yeah. It's like they expect you to already be good at it."

Ram looked up from his cup. "They do," he said simply.

Emma blinked. "Wait, really?"

"Employers highly value Smartness," Ram said. "Even if they don't use that term. They're looking for people who can think clearly, adapt fast, follow through, and lead when needed—people who know how to make things happen."

Jack frowned. "So, they want Smartness... but expect us to figure it out ourselves?"

Ram nodded. "Exactly. They expect you to develop it on the job—or find your own way to get there."

Emma exhaled. "But what if you're new? What if no one ever taught you this?"

Ram leaned in. "Unless a mentor or colleague takes an interest in teaching you, you're on your own. That's why building networks, both at work and outside work, isn't optional. It's how most people learn the ways of the world. Like lion cubs learning to hunt, you need others to show you how. It's much harder and takes much longer to figure these out on your own."

He let that land, then continued. "But here's the part no one tells you: if no one steps in to help, you're already behind. Also, if you don't develop and learn to use it by other means, no one will step in to help you. Employers value Smartness, but they expect you to show up with it. If you're a new graduate, or even a mid-career employee who never invested the time and money to build it, you're at a huge disadvantage. Not because you're not capable, but because you haven't developed your Smartness or learned how to apply it when it counts."

He added, "You're expected to either show up ready—or get ready fast, if you want to be successful."

Emma – Waiting to Be Taught

Emma looked out the window. "In college, teachers came to us. The class was assigned. The textbook was available at the university bookstore or Amazon. The professor led the way. Even the study group just happened."

She paused. "But now? It's crickets."

Ram nodded. "That's the trap. You're still waiting to be taught."

She sighed. "And I'm starting to realize… no one's coming to teach us."

Ram leaned back. "Correct. You are the student, and you have to find the teacher. Sometimes, you have to become your own. And when you can't? You may have to form your own study group."

Jack – Passive No More

Jack swirled the last sip of his coffee. "It's wild. We spent six figures on college without blinking. But now, if something costs more than fifty bucks, people take a hard pass."

Ram raised an eyebrow. "That's a student mindset. Looking for something for nothing."

Emma frowned. "You mean like free webinars, pirated PDFs, shared passwords, and YouTube tutorials?"

"Yes," Ram said. "A lot of marketing promises free—but free still costs you. People think they're saving money, but they're actually giving up something more valuable: their time, energy, and focus. And instead of using those to grow, they spend it chasing tips, shortcuts, and secrets that don't build real capability. The ones who invest in their own development, the ones who put real skin in the game, use that same time, energy, and focus on personal development, to build real capabilities. They learn faster. Apply more. Achieve more. Progress, like money, compounds. A few years in, they've pulled far ahead of the ones still chasing free."

Ram continued, "It dumbfounds me that most people who spent hundreds of thousands on a degree won't invest even a fraction of that amount on personal development. Everybody should set aside a portion of their annual income for personal development. Remember, you are your most important project, and your best investment. If you won't invest in yourself, who else do you think will?"

Emma looked down. She knew she'd spent more on a single textbook than she'd ever spent on personal development. She also realized why most people stop learning after college—it's no longer scheduled, structured, or rewarded. And without a syllabus or a professor to answer to, most people drift. Not because they're lazy. But because no one's watching.

"The world doesn't reward what you know," Ram said. "It rewards what you can do with it. And being willing to invest in that ability? That's the difference between drifting and achieving. This is particularly important for people who feel unsuccessful or stuck."

Jack nodded slowly. He was done chasing "free." This wasn't about tuition anymore. It was about responsibility. If he didn't invest in himself, who would?

That night, he pulled Ram's book off his shelf and let it fall open where he'd last dog-eared a page. He didn't need to search. The line was already underlined in pen:

"Many mistake complacency for contentment. They tell themselves they're satisfied, when deep down, they're just avoiding effort. If you want more but do nothing, that's not contentment. That's lazy complacence disguised as acceptance."

Jack stared at the words. They didn't feel abstract anymore. They felt aimed. Because he'd been doing exactly that—telling himself it was fine, when really, he'd just been stalling. Waiting for some clarity to arrive and make the next step obvious. But clarity hadn't come. And comfort had quietly become a cage.

He flipped a few more pages, and another sentence caught his eye:

> *"Ninety-six percent of unsuccessful smart people knew what to do, but didn't act."*

Ninety-six. Not fifty. Not seventy. Almost all of them.

Jack sat with that. It wasn't that they didn't know. It was that they didn't act—or didn't act effectively.

And then it landed—maybe for the first time: *It's easier to do nothing.*

Easier to say later.

Easier to keep reading than to start doing.

He closed the book, not because he was done, but because he was ready. Ready to stop telling himself it would somehow just work out.

That night, he made a new rule for himself. Ten percent of his income—every year—would go toward personal development. Not just learning more, but becoming more. Not just gaining knowledge, but applying it.

Because the gap between knowing and doing wasn't going to close on its own.

From Assigned Learning to Self-Driven Growth

In school, learning was scheduled. Professors taught. Feedback came built-in. Study groups formed automatically. The real world doesn't work like that.

> *No one's coming to teach you. If you want to grow, you'll have to seek it out.*

Build your own group. Find mentors. Make friends who challenge you. And be willing to invest—time, energy, and money—into your own personal development.

Smartness doesn't get handed to you. It gets developed—by you.

And the sooner you take ownership, the faster you will bridge the gap between your smarts and aspirations.

CHAPTER 21

RAM'S GIFT

Ram had promised them clarity, not comfort. A couple of weeks later, he invited them to meet over coffee again. This time, not as mentees looking for direction, but as individuals ready to take ownership.

They sat at a quiet corner table in the same café, coffees in hand. Ram didn't open with a question. He pulled two envelopes from his bag and slid them across the table.

Emma looked excited and asked. "What's this?"

"Call it a graduation gift," he said. "Not from college, but from the phase you just outgrew."

Both Emma and Jack opened their enveloped. Inside was a single printed page with a quote at the top that read:

"Intelligence is your engine. Smartness is your steering."

Underneath was a list of their strongest enablers, their sneakiest disablers, and the mixed Smartness Factors they'd wrestled with the most. These were from their *Smartness Assessment* Report.

Emma's Quiet Breakthrough

Emma glanced down at her sheet. Three "mixed" factors glared back at her like a warning light: *Self-Advocacy, Outward Confidence,* and *Personal Autonomy.*

Ram didn't sugarcoat it. "Emma, you're skilled. You're thoughtful. But you're playing defense with your own value."

She frowned. "I don't want to come off as… showy."

"You won't," he said. "But you're acting like someone who's waiting to be selected. And that's not how this game works."

He handed her a plain white card.

Your Assignment: The Visibility Drill

Over the next 7 days:

1. Choose one idea, result, or insight you've contributed to your team—no matter how small.
2. Find a way to make it visible—in a team meeting, Slack update, 1-on-1, or email.
3. Frame it as a value, not vanity. Anchor it in "why it matters."

Then reflect:

1. What resistance came up?
2. What felt different about being visible?
3. What changed—if anything?

Ram leaned forward. "Christine from HQ got promoted last quarter. You know why?"

Emma shook her head.

"She wasn't the smartest. But she was the most visible. People can't reward what they can't see."

Emma stared at the card. She didn't want the spotlight—but maybe she didn't need it. Maybe she just needed to stop hiding.

Jack's Micro Momentum

Jack looked at his sheet and saw *Action Orientation* staring back like a dare.

Ram didn't say anything right away. Just waited.

"I keep thinking," Jack said, "that once I find the right angle, I'll move."

Ram nodded. "Thinking is how you get clarity. But doing is how you get traction. Remember, Action Orientation disables 96% of unsuccessful people to varying extents."

He slid over a tiny notebook. On the front was written: *Jack's Momentum Log.*

Jack's Assignment: Ten Actions in Ten Days

Each morning:

1. Write down one action you can complete in under 10 minutes, something bold, specific, and slightly uncomfortable.
2. Do it before noon.
   - Reach out for feedback.
   - Pitch an idea.
   - Share something on LinkedIn.
3. At night, log your responses to one question: *What did I do and what did I learn?*

Ram leaned in. "The goal isn't outcomes. It's to develop a rhythm and build momentum. Your brain's stuck in strategy mode. Let your body move."

Jack nodded. It sounded too simple. Which is exactly why he hadn't done it yet.

The Real Turning Point for Emma and Jack

They didn't announce their progress. They didn't need to. Emma had learned how to speak through action—and then let her impact be seen with confidence, not hesitation. Jack had learned how to stop waiting for certainty and start creating clarity with his voice.

Neither of them had figured it all out. But their efforts had momentum now.

They didn't question every piece of Ram's guidance. Not anymore. They had seen enough of it work. And maybe that was its own kind of wisdom—earned, not argued.

Emma stopped waiting for the perfect question. Jack stopped perfecting things in private. They acted—imperfectly, quietly, but consistently. They were learning by doing. And in the process, they were developing their own judgment—making smarter decisions, faster.

They weren't just applying somebody else's advice anymore. For most of their lives, they had followed instructions—from parents, from teachers, from people who meant well.

But developing Smartness was different. They weren't doing it for approval. They were developing it by themselves—autonomously and deliberately—to keep growing it for the rest of their lives, and to have it serve them for the rest of their lives.

It was a significant shift. One that was starting to deliver results they could feel.

Unlike people who dismiss old truths because they weren't backed by a PhD or published by a modern university—Harvard, for example, is only about 400 years old—they were beginning to understand something deeper. Human civilization has existed for over 10,000 years. Wisdom didn't start at Harvard, Stanford or some other modern university as some would like to believe.

Human wisdom is much older. Passed down over thousands of years. Refined through experience, not research citations.

"Smartness is like wisdom—developed and refined through experience in real life, not research in a lab."

Not invented in a lab, but developed through observation, practice and adaptation. Lived. It's in the fabric of how people learn, adapt, grow, and achieve greater success, together.

Emma and Jack weren't chasing motivation. They were building momentum. And that momentum was starting to compound—into real traction, visible results, and something more lasting:

Greater confidence and greater success.

CHAPTER 22

TAKEOFF

Progress rarely announces itself. It sneaks in through one email sent, one idea shared, one moment of discomfort faced with a little less hesitation.

Emma and Jack weren't transformed overnight. But something had shifted. The friction they once avoided was turning into motion. And motion, over time, becomes momentum.

This chapter isn't about applause. This chapter isn't about applause. It's about taking initiative followed by action.

Emma – The Real Win (Slack-Style)

Emma had spotted the issue two weeks ago. The dashboard that sales and ops used every day had a broken filter, something small, but disruptive. People had grumbled about it, but no one had fixed it.

She didn't ask for permission. She cloned the dashboard, tested a few fixes, ran simulations to make sure nothing else would break, and quietly implemented the cleaner version.

Once it was stable, she posted a quick note in the *#team-ops* Slack channel:

"*Hey all, noticed a bug in the dashboard filter. Took a stab at a fix. Let me know if it improves things or if I missed anything.*"

Maya replied almost instantly: "YES! This fixes the lag. Thank you 🙌"

Two others added comments. Her manager reacted with a 👍 and followed up later during the sync: "Shoutout to Emma. Fixing that dashboard bug saved everyone time last week."

Emma didn't beam. She didn't downplay it either. She just said, "Glad it helped."

She had created value—and made it visible.

Ram's earlier words came back to her: *"Credibility is earned twice."*

This wasn't self-promotion. It was professional visibility. She didn't need to shout to be seen. But she did need to show up.

Jack – From Thinking to Trusted

Jack had been in the role for a few months now. The company was small, the projects messy, and decisions moved fast. It should have been a dream job for someone with ideas. But for Jack, it had been… quieter than expected.

Not because he didn't have insights. But because he wasn't sharing them. In meetings, he'd craft thoughtful suggestions in his head but say nothing. He told himself it was humility. But it was really hesitation. Then Ram's voice came back to him:

"Self-Advocacy doesn't mean bragging. It means not leaving your value invisible."

The next Monday, a product rollout was at risk. The team debated timing, logistics, and sequence. Jack listened, thought, paused… and then spoke:

"We could stage the launch. Backend this week, UI next. It won't solve everything, but it'll unblock the engineering sprint."

There was a moment of silence. Then a nod. Then more nods.

His manager said, "Good call. Can you outline the rollout logic in Slack?"

Jack wrote up a brief thread, attached a diagram, and hit send. No overthinking. No apologies.

Later that day, someone from the design team replied, "This clarified so much. Thanks, Jack."

That night, he opened his journal and wrote: *"I stopped waiting to be invited. I started showing up with value."*

He realized that he hadn't just spoken up—he'd made a Communication & Presentation Choice. Not just what to say, but *how* to say it. Concise. Actionable. Delivered at the right moment, in the right space—where it would be noticed and used."

Smartness wasn't about always having the best idea. It was about making sure your ideas *landed*.

Ram had told him once:

> *"People trust what they see and hear—
> so show it. Say it. And say it well."*

That's what Jack was learning to do. He wasn't trying to sound brilliant. He was just being useful—and making it visible.

And that, it turned out, was what teams trusted most.

They didn't announce their progress. They didn't need to.

Emma had learned to speak through action—and then let her impact be seen, with confidence instead of hesitation. Jack had stopped waiting for permission and started creating clarity through presence and contribution.

Neither of them had solved everything. But both had moved far enough to know they weren't stuck anymore.

Enough to speak.

Enough to be heard.

Enough to trust their own momentum.

It wasn't mastery. It wasn't arrival. But it was the most important part of any real change: takeoff.

And soon, they'd discover that the smartest thing they could do with their growth… was share it.

CHAPTER 23

SIX MONTHS LATER

The little café was louder than usual. At the far end, a group had taken over four tables—coffee cups, notebooks, diagrams, and side conversations. Emma glanced around: Jack, Sofia, and a few others from other parts of their lives.

This was their Smartness Circle.

Ram had introduced them to a few more people serious about growing. The rules were simple: share what's working, what's not working, and what you're doing to improve.

No lectures. Just real challenges. Real growth.

One person unpacked a pitch that went sideways. Another shared how they finally took a risk they'd been putting off. Nobody tried to impress. They came to learn.

Emma asked sharper questions than she would've six months ago. Jack spotted a pattern others had missed. They didn't pretend to have all the answers. Together, they were learning to see, listen, think, and act with more clarity.

Ram wasn't at the table that day. He didn't need to be—Smartness had taken root. This was just one of hundreds of peer-led Smartness Circles—people developing and using Smartness to grow, contribute, and thrive—in real life, around the world.

CHAPTER 24

THE REAL BEGINNING

Emma stood at the edge of the conference room, laptop in hand. No one had told her what to do—but she'd already drafted a follow-up, flagged a risk, and pulled in someone who could help. Six months ago, she would've waited to be asked. Today, she acted. Not perfectly. But with purpose.

Jack, across town, had just blocked his calendar—not to look busy, but to protect space for growth. A 30-minute window every Thursday. One Smartness capability at a time. Quiet progress. No announcement needed.

They weren't done growing. Far from it. But they were no longer waiting for permission.

Smartness wasn't a trick or a tip. It was a capability they were building—deliberately, in motion.

Because the truth is: success in the real world doesn't go to the smartest. It goes to the ones who learn, adapt, and keep applying what they've got—especially when it's hard. That's Smartness. And it's yours to build.

"You're not here to prove you're ready. You're here to become ready."

This isn't the end. This is your beginning.

INTERLUDE
What Is a Successful Life?

Success isn't a fixed destination—it's an evolving ideal. Everyone defines it differently. We all chase it, and sometimes fall short. That doesn't mean we stop trying.

It's like the ideal of always telling the truth. You might fall short once—but that doesn't mean you give up on being honest. You keep striving to be honest.

That's where the Achievement Cycle becomes your ally. Whether you hit your goal today or not, every loop—Assess, Target, Act, Reflect—sharpens your ability to succeed. With each pass, you build the Smartness and experience needed to close the gap between who you are and who you're striving to become.

A successful life isn't one big win—a home run, a touchdown, or a three-pointer.

Instead, it's progress. Getting to first base. Moving the ball down the field. Advancing up the court.

Life is a series of loops. A life where you keep learning, adjusting, and moving forward.

> *"Success isn't about getting it perfect. It's about getting better every time—and striving until you attain the success you seek."*

ABOUT THE AUTHOR

Ram V. Iyer is an MIT-educated engineer, five-time entrepreneur, and former venture capitalist who has spent his life exploring one powerful question:

Why do so many people with advantages—like intelligence, credentials, wealth, or skills—underachieve?

His journey from success to setback and back again shaped a mission to help smart people succeed—not by becoming smarter, but by learning to use what they already have more effectively.

Ram's voice is grounded in lived experience. He's worked at Fortune 100 global corporations like Boeing and Lucent, served as a venture capitalist in Silicon Valley, and launched startups on multiple continents. He's won, lost, and come back stronger. *MONEY* magazine once called him "The Comeback Kid." The lessons in this book are hard-earned, deeply personal, and delivered MIT-style: direct, no-nonsense, and practical.

He's been invited to speak at MIT, Harvard, and Princeton, and to over a dozen top-tier alumni organizations including Wharton, Ross, Booth, Kellogg, Dartmouth, and Berkeley. He served as President of both the MIT South Asian Alumni Association and the MIT Club of Princeton. His work has been featured in *Money*, *Fortune*, *CIO*, *CFO*, and other leading media, and his clients have included Fortune 100 companies.

Ram's turning point came when he realized that advantages like intelligence alone aren't enough to ensure success—not for him, and not for the thousands of smart professionals he's met. That insight led to his identification of the **Advantage Illusion**—the false belief that intelligence or credentials automatically ensure success—and to the creation of the **Smartness Factors**, the **Smartness Assessment**, and the **Achievement Cycle**.

He defines **Smartness** as the ability to apply one's intelligence and advantages adaptively in various contexts to achieve real-world success. It's not a fixed trait. It's a capability that anybody—at any age, in any role—can develop, strengthen, and use to create better outcomes.

Ram founded **The Smartness Institute** (www.mySmartness.com) to help people everywhere turn potential into progress. His tools have now helped thousands become more effective, intentional, and successful.

This is the book smart professionals didn't know they needed—until they saw what's been missing. It's a practical, straight-talking guide for smart people who are stuck—and ready to start achieving more.

APPLYING THIS BOOK IN THE REAL WORLD... TODAY

How to Align What You Think, Say, and Do So You Get Results

You've read Emma and Jack's story. You've hopefully seen yourself in some of those scenes. You've probably realized that being smart isn't enough. What matters is how you leverage who you are and use what you have.

That's what real-world alignment is all about. It's when your thoughts, actions, and communication actually match what the moment calls for—being context-aware, role-flexible, and outcome-focused.

This doesn't happen automatically. Most people develop one area but neglect the others. For example:

- Some think well but never act—overthinking without execution, which leads to no meaningful results.
- Some act fast but miss the point—impulsive action without clear intention, which fails to create real outcomes.
- Others over-communicate loudly but with little clarity or meaning, creating noise that echoes but produces no progress.

Such misalignment causes smart people to stall or even fail.

What Is Real-World Alignment?

Real-world alignment is simple. It happens when your mindsets, behaviors, and interactions are all working together with what your situation requires, not just what you're used to doing.

It's not about being perfect. It's about being tuned in, responsive, and intentional.

It's the difference between spinning your wheels and actually making progress.

Many graduates don't chase their own goals. They chase someone else's version of success.

If you don't define what success looks like for you, you may spend your life climbing a ladder someone else designed and built—only to realize it's leaning against the wrong wall. Smartness requires ownership.

> *If your ambitions are borrowed,*
> *your success will be hollow.*

Five Alignment Shifts You Can Make Right Now

1. **Stop over-prepping. Start acting.**

    You don't need perfect plans. You need thoughtful action. Real-world alignment means knowing when to pause and when to move.

    Emma once spent three days crafting the perfect slide deck. Later, she realized that a three-line email would have moved the project faster.

    Jack held back from applying to a role because his résumé felt unfinished. Someone else with half his experience got the job.

2. **Lead with clarity, not noise.**

    Gen Z is great at expression, but real-world influence comes from simplicity, timing, and tone. Say what matters. At the right time. In the right way.

In a team meeting, Emma pitched five ideas in great detail and lost the room. The intern presented one punchy idea and it landed.

Jack updated his manager on every little task. Then he learned to provide highlights and outcomes instead and got noticed for it.

3. **Trust your instincts, but test them.**

    Emotional intelligence is a gift. But feelings aren't facts. Real-world alignment means combining empathy with evidence before you make a move.

    Emma felt her coworker didn't like her. When she checked in, she learned he was just overwhelmed with deadlines.

    Jack wanted to quit after a tough week. Ram asked, "What data are you using to make that decision?" Jack paused and decided to stay.

4. **Build boldness through small wins.**

    Confidence grows from execution, not applause. Want to feel ready? Do something. Then do it again. Action creates alignment.

    Emma stopped waiting to feel ready. She took a messy first shot and it led to her first real project win.

    Jack finally presented his idea in a team huddle. They didn't cheer, but they implemented it. That was enough.

5. **Don't confuse variety with progress.**

    You're wired for exploration. That's great. But real success comes when curiosity is paired with follow-through. Finish things. That's where the impact is.

    Emma loved starting projects, but Ram pointed out she finished very few of them. That changed her mindset.

    Jack kept bouncing between career ideas. One day, he stuck with one long enough to see it through. That's when things began to shift.

One Final Nudge

Many graduates swing between "I'm not good enough" and "I'm better than everyone."

Smartness is the third path: *"I know who I am—and I know what I'm still learning."*

You don't need a perfect career plan. You need real-world alignment.

You already have the intelligence and knowledge. This book helped you see them.

Now it's time to sync them and get results.

> *The world doesn't reward potential. It rewards progress and results. And those come from showing up in sync with who you are and what the moment calls for.*
>
> *You're a graduate. Grab life by the horns with Smartness. Success will follow.*

The Smartness Institute

Helping Smart People Become More Successful—for Life

Smartness isn't just something you read about, it's something you build and use every day. It is behaviorally expressed and situationally applied. That's why I created **The Smartness Institute**: a global resource hub to help smart people like you develop the mindsets, behaviors, skills and capabilities that drive real-world achievement.

At The Smartness Institute, you'll find:

- Practical frameworks and micro-courses to grow your Smartness
- Deep dives into the Smartness Factors
- The *Smartness Assessment* and personalized development plans
- Tools for leaders, managers, and coaches to help others close their *Smartness Gap*
- A growing community of achievers who are getting unstuck—and moving forward
- The latest thinking and resources to develop and use your Smartness

If this book made you think differently, The Smartness Institute is your next step.

Visit **www.mySmartness.com** to start your Smartness journey today.

Resources for Greater Success

You just read *Graduated… But Not Ready for the Real World*

You've seen Emma and Jack begin their journey after graduation—into the real world.

If Emma's story felt familiar, it means you've felt the frustration of being smart yet stuck. That's not failure—it's the *Smartness Gap*.

If Jack's story hit closer to home, maybe you've experienced the silence—doing everything right, but still feeling invisible or unsure where to go next.

This parable isn't the full system—it's the wake-up call.

Now it's your turn. Start building your Smartness.

> *"Desire is cheap. Most people want success—but drift through life—because they lack a compelling reason behind their desire for success. Desire isn't enough.*
>
> *Millions express their desire to become millionaires or CEOs, but the ones who succeed are the ones who know why the goal matters to them, and are willing to do whatever success demands."*

Take the Smartness Assessment

Uncover the real reasons you're not getting the results you want. Some will surprise you.

www.MySmartness.com/*assessments*

Free for new grads—normally $198. Use discount code: ***NewGradBook*** at checkout.

You'll get an email with your *Smartness Assessment Report* on how you stack up on the 21 Smartness Factors within minutes. It's been taken by thousands of graduates from across the world – from California to Australia.

What you'll learn:

- Your top Smartness Enablers (what's already working for you)
- Your top Smartness Disablers (what's quietly holding you back)
- Clear, personalized insights based on real data
- Optional: unlock your full Smartness Archetype and deeper reports

> *"You don't need to become more intelligent to become more successful. You need to get smarter at applying who you already are."*

Go Deeper with the Companion Books & Playbook

If you're ready to grow faster:

1. Read the full book

How Smart People Can Become More Successful

That isn't a parable—it's the deep dive. You'll get the full Smartness system, real-world strategies, and step-by-step tools to convert insight into achievement.

2. Use the Smartness Playbook

A hands-on guide packed with worksheets, prompts, and practices to help you apply Smartness every day. It is a companion book to the *How Smart People Can Become More Successful* book. It'll walk you through gaining clarity on your 'why', understanding your enablers, disablers and mixed, worksheets to help you leverage or mitigate them, and track your progress.

You can find both at: MySmartness.com/books

* * * * * * * * * * * * * * * * * * * *

Smartness Circles: Growth-Focused, Not Commerce-Focused

We're building Smartness Circles in cities and professions—small, invite-only peer groups for people committed to applying Smartness in real life. These aren't sales funnels or coaching programs. No pitching. No promotions. Just real people developing Smartness—together, in real life.

Every self-policed Smartness Circle begins with a clear pledge: commit to personal Smartness development and mutual support. Members must sign a Code of Conduct—zero tolerance for agenda-pushing or prospecting. Violators are banned—permanently. One strike. You're out.

I'm creating these Smartness Circles to connect people, not to monetize them. While I will offer paid Smartness Camps and advanced coaching separately, Smartness Circles are strictly for personal development—not for prospecting, coaching, or client-building.

Want to start or join a Smartness Circle in your city? Request an intro at:

www.MySmartness.com/SmartnessCircle

Smartness Camps

Live, immersive experiences where you can work with others to develop and apply your Smartness in real-world situations. Each session focuses on one or more of the Smartness Factors. While I lead them, they aren't lectures—they're live labs to develop your capabilities and accelerate your success. Learn more at: www.MySmartness.com/SmartnessCamps

Don't Wait for a Teacher to Find You

In college, you met teachers in assigned classrooms. Courses were structured. Help was scheduled. There were teaching assistants.

In real life? **No one's coming to teach you.**

You have to find your teachers—and join or form your own study groups, just like you may have done in school. However, just be smart enough not to chase *free*—or waste money on snake oil salespeople.

That is also what Smartness is: knowing how to seek insights, ask better questions, and surround yourself with people who can raise your game.

Get Mentored (When You're Ready)

If this book resonated and you want more hands-on guidance, I offer limited one-on-one Smartness Mentoring—for people serious about change.

This isn't a course or a pitch. It's personalized mentoring designed to help you close your *Smartness Gap* and accelerate your progress. Quiet. Focused. Real.

If you're ready to do the work, I'll meet you there.

Learn more at: MySmartness.com/mentoring

Don't Go It Alone

Smartness grows faster when built with others.
- Join a Smartness Circle if you want to stay local
- Join a Smartness coaching group if you want expert guidance
- Attend a cohort-based course
- Explore and share real-world Smartness stories at *MySmartness.com/stories*

You've gotten as far as you can with what you've got.

To go farther—and higher—you must develop and apply your Smartness. What you do with your Smartness determines what kind of life you'll build.

> *"Intelligence and your college education might help you avoid becoming a loser—but without Smartness, you'll never become an Achiever."*

You've graduated from college. Now graduate into a life of success and fulfillment—with Smartness.

You've gotten as far as you can with what you've got. To go farther and higher, you must develop and apply your Smartness.

"Intelligence and your college education might help you avoid becoming a loser—but without Smartness, you'll never become an Achiever."